A Place That I Love

A Place That I Love

A Tour Driver's Perspective of Mackinac Island

Walter Kitter

To order additional copies of this book, contact:
Xlibris
1-888-795-4274
www.Xlibris.com
Orders@Xlibris.com
546384

CONTENTS

Introduction ix
Downtown 1
The Barns...7
Night Barn 11
The Farriers...13
The Kitchen 19
The Kings of the Island (the Horse)....................................22
Lilacs and the Lilac Festival...30
Lilac Queens of the Past 33
Sainte Anne's Church...35
Round Island Lighthouse...43
Dr. William Beaumont 49
The Fur Trade 52
John Jacob Astor...61
Some Facts 64
Courthouse..65
The Forts...67
The War of 1812 at Fort Mackinac..................................... 80
The Other Season 94
April...100
The Grand Hotel 102
West Bluff...113
Annex...123
The Governor's Summer Residence 127
Some Facts 130
Anne's Tablet...132
East Bluff...134
Cemeteries...138
Geological Features...141
Pictures...152
Some Other Places for Pictures..154
Bibliography 159
Index 165

I would like to take this opportunity to thank my family and my friends who helped me as we talked through problems. Whether they know it or not, they all helped in their own special way. This book would not be possible without the help of the people who supplied the pictures: the Michigan Department of Transportation, Steven Blair, and Dale Peterson. I also want to take the time to thank all the wonderful people who have volunteered to be readers, just seeing how this book reads. I know my friends are just as excited as I am to finally be at this stage.

INTRODUCTION

I have driven a lot of teams in my eleven years as a tour driver for Mackinac Island Carriage Tours. I really enjoyed this job; doing it was more like living the dream. The history, the horses, and most importantly, the customers made my day go by so fast. I researched the information for my tour. There was no way I was going to answer questions on someone else's material. My tour was always changing from year to year with the research I would do in the off-season, for both the tour and for this book. I had to make this my own tour; for some reason, I had to have some form of ownership of the material if I was going to do my job right. With the research, I sometimes found the stories behind the facts a little more interesting than some of the facts themselves. Really, I could not tell the whole story though, because the customers would miss out on some interesting facts about other sites, which were just as important.

One rainy, wet, cold day, one of those days you could have been duck hunting (all you would have needed were call, decoys, a boat and a lab, and a shotgun, of course, and you would have been set—it does not get any better than that), sitting downtown, rain dripping off my carriage onto my head, as I leaned forward, watching my team, Spot and Roy, I got the idea for this book. I wanted to tell the story behind the facts. As Paul Harvey would say, "Now you know the rest of the story." So now I had this idea for this book, but I already had a problem: what was I going to do for pictures? By this time, I had finally made it to the ticket office.

Again I was staring out over Spot and Roy, in obvious deep thought; you could see that the squirrels were really running around on the wheel in my head. One of the customers that were going to be on my tour asked, "What are you in deep thought about?" I explained to him this book idea. I needed to figure out what it was I was going to do for pictures. Well, he brought up that the frame for pictures was the two horses in front of me. What a cool idea. Problem solved. So we were talking, Spot and Roy were getting their drink of water, then along came Dr. Bill. He interrupted our conversation and explained to the customers that their driver was a thespian. He had me with that one. I had to write the word down where I would not lose it so I could look it up. I had an idea what it was; it had something to do with acting. I knew he was paying me a compliment. I just wanted to make sure I was right.

This has been a labor of love—I love the island, and I love to write. This book takes you on a journey, a journey through time, just like one of the tours will. My hope is like on the tour, that everybody who reads it enjoys it.

Downtown

Parked in the middle of Main Street, at different locations throughout downtown, all the way to the ticket office, are the tour carriages. They are in the middle so traffic can pass on either side of them. The drivers are watching over their teams, making sure that their horses behave themselves. Making sure that all the drivers are all right is a man you will see riding a bicycle around, Mr. Dick Ruluson, also known as Big Arrow. He is always telling you where to go. You will see him riding his bike up and down Main Street and up and down the boulevard, checking on the drivers as they pass. The bicycle that he rides is a speed bike with a porter basket. In that porter basket will probably be his rain gear and maybe some spare harness parts that may be needed at some point in time. Also adorning this bicycle are umpteen Mackinac Island bicycle licenses, one of the requirements of owning a bike on Mackinac Island. He is tall and lanky. He has a gray beard, and he wears blue jeans, a T-shirt, glasses, a radio on his hip, and a ball cap with the Carriage Tours logo on it, or he may be hanging out in the yard at Chambers Corner or Market Street and Cadott, watching the carriages as they come downhill to get in line for the ticket office once again.

For about the last sixteen years or so, Mr. Dick Ruluson keeps watch on the carriages, making sure carriages go where they are needed. He is in constant contact with the ticket office and the barn. Sometimes he is stationary at either end of Main Street or at Woodfill Memorial, taking notes, and sometimes he is cruising Main Street, making notes of which carriage is where. It is his job to spot problems before they happen. He also sends the carriages to where they are needed to pick up the next group that is coming in from the ferry or a group that may be scheduled out of the many hotels on the island.

As we are coming down the boulevard, he is looking over the harness, the hookup, and the horses. He will stop us if something appears to be wrong and does some barn work to fix the problem. He will pull off loose shoes if they need to be pulled. He knows who the veteran drivers are and who the rookie drivers are. He knows the drivers and the horses very well. He has a sharp eye for detail. For the past five years as a driver for the company, I am glad that Dick Ruluson is around, not only because he is able to fix a problem, but also because if Dick is at Woodfill Memorial, the day is going to be busy, and it will go real fast. We will be going short to the ticket office, "straight to where the money is at," the day will be busy and fast. When the days are slow, he will be at Woodfill Memorial, letting the ticket office know where the next carriage is at. More than likely, on slow days, he will send us around the beach. Sometimes they will need a carriage right away, so he will send the next driver coming down from Surrey Hill straight to the ticket office. If we are coming down the boulevard and he is not at the Woodfill Memorial, he will more than likely be down on Main Street, because it is a slow day and the drivers are lined up downtown. The problems will more than likely be downtown, where bikes have to be moved because they are in the way of the carriages. If I am parked correctly, there will be room for my carriage, one going one way and one going the other way. The day is going to be long, and *tiddledywinks*, trying to get our thumbs to rotate in opposite directions, are in order.

My personal dealings with Dick were often when I had done something wrong, or when the ticket office needed me to be somewhere else and while coming down the hill, I would notice something wrong with my harness or hookup and I would ask Dick to check it out. Most of my mistakes were when he was on the job for the first day, like when I left the barn for the first tour in my own buggy and in the beginning of the season. The first time I ever had to deal with Dick was my first day as a tour driver. I had a sharp memory, and I had an idea of the spots designated as stops while lined up downtown. Being excited, I was talking while he was explaining. He told me that I was not in the barnyard anymore and to listen. I listened, and we had a few problems. Another encounter with Dick was my first day back for the season, and I was coming downtown for the first trip of the day, coming down the hill, when I was told to "get in line for the Arnold Line and stay put." What he wanted me to do was park in front of the Thunderbird and wait for the next boat. When I got downtown, there was a carriage being loaded with a tour group that had pulled out. Seeing this, I was thinking I was supposed to pick up the rest of the group. I pulled in, thinking there were people to still pick up. To my surprise, there was none. Like clockwork, Dick rolled up alongside my carriage and calmly asked, "What part of stay put don't you understand, Walt? Now go around and come down Astor Street, and get in line and stay put."

There were a couple of times when I was the first tour driver to arrive for the season. I was the ticket officer, the loader, and the tour driver. I would do probably two, maybe three, tours a day. I never had to pay attention to the arrow that was placed at Chambers Corner, because the ticket office was not open yet. A couple of times on the first day, the ticket office would be open. I would be coming down from Surrey Hill after my first trip of the day, and not paying attention to the goofy arrow pointing for me to go around the beach, I would go straight to the ticket office. Like clockwork, Dick would come rolling alongside my carriage on his bicycle, asking if I had any intentions of paying attention to the arrow. I would explain that I was doing tours before the ticket office was open. Then he would see if they needed me right away or if they wanted me to go around the beach like I was supposed to in the beginning.

I do know that he does appreciate the drivers who will pay attention to what is going on with their teams, because if they are paying attention to the teams like they should, it is less of a hassle for him in the long run. Most of the time, Dick will not hold a team. His job is to respond to trouble if there is any. If he was holding a team, he would not be able to respond to the problem like he is supposed to.

Just as important was another person. His name was Joe Bazinaw, also known as Snapper. He has since passed away. This man would be walking up and down Main Street, checking on the drivers, asking them if they needed to get down and stretch their legs or go to the bathroom. Snapper was allowed to hold for the drivers. He was a very experienced person and was a nice person to talk with. He was also very humble. He was always in constant contact with the ticket office. Most of the time, with exception of slow days, when walking back to his or her team, the driver would not have to walk very far. Snapper would move the carriage up the middle of Main Street as the carriages in front of him moved up. Someone always had to keep an eye on the team and hold the lines.

Most of the time, that is the only break the drivers will get, with the exception of the ticket office and at Surrey Hill. The ticket office is the command center for the company during the day. It is very busy. This is where the tour buggies are told where to go, which driver is doing what, and what they are going to do when they get there. Kitty sometimes will answer the phone when Mike and Ed are busy loading people for the public tour or watering the horses. She runs that ticket office, and Mike and Ed usually run the livery board.

Ed Holman stood about six feet and five inches, with gray hair. He wore mirrored sunglasses out of the seventies. He was a front man for Elvis at one time and was also a tour guide for the historical battlefield at Gettysburg. He liked his history and was well versed on it. He obviously also liked his Elvis Presley. He had a high standard when it came to the tour. I really hoped I met that bar. It was Ed who introduced me to a series of books written by Allan Eckert, the Winning of America Series, following Manifest Destiny across the United States. While in the kitchen one time, Ed saw that I had received my absentee ballot in the mail. He told me, "I will personally drive you down to Chicago and drive you around to all the precincts so you can vote for your man." I just died laughing; it was so funny. He told me about Governor Rod Blagojevich and how corrupt he was and how he was going to prison two years before it happened.

The ticket office is also where the liveries are being dispatched. If we get a trip out of the park, we will call into livery base, let them know for how long, how many people, and whether cash or credit. Some of the times, livery drivers will be booked through the day, and that is a good day for being busy, and the day for me usually flies by. The ticket office is where they also water and apply fly spray to the teams of horses that are downtown. Twenty passenger carriages get the majority of their water and fly spray during the season. They will also hold the team for the driver.

I am trying to paint a picture that the ticket office is a very busy place and sometimes people are doing three things at the same time and that the only way it works is if everyone pitches in and does their part.

THE BARNS

Some of the hardest behind-the-scene works go in the barnyard. Each of the three barns in the yard has someone running them, as well as barn 4, which is only open between Memorial Day and Labor Day. For instance, the man running the Taxi Barn is responsible for the cleaning of that barn and getting all the day's switches ready for when the cabs come in for their switches. He also has to switch each of the teams as they come. Any horse that needs to be shod will, at some point during the day, be shod and ready to go for the day. During the day, he gives haircuts to any of the horses that may need it. He has to clean the barn, fill the hay shoots, and feed the grain. He also has to help put up hay as well.

The man running the middle barn, or the three-horse barn, is responsible for the cleaning of that barn and getting the work teams ready. Drivers usually help clean the middle barn in the morning. Switch teams are cleaned and harnessed, and he makes sure that all the drivers show up for work. The teams that are assigned to the drivers are clean, harnessed, and ready to go on tour. When "Buggy on the hill!" is yelled, that is time for the drivers who are the ones wanting to be first out of the barn to hook up in the three-horse barn. They have to clean the barns, fill the hay shoots, and feed the grain.

In Big Barn, the tour drivers will have their teams harnessed and ready to go by eight fifteen, unless there is an early hookup. Hooking up a team of horses is a team effort. You have barnmen putting neck yokes on and connecting the inside lines, then some are hooking the horses to the carriages, and you have one barnman washing the carriage. The process is repeated an hour later in the three-horse barn. The barnmen are responsible for the cleaning of the barn, getting the work teams ready, taking the manure from all the barns to the dump, where it is put into the compost pile. This is where all recyclable material and waste from the island are hauled. They are also getting the switch teams ready. They have to clean the barns, fill the hay shoots, and feed the grain.

Between Memorial Day and Labor Day, the company runs switch teams. A driver will receive a fresh team of horses about halfway through the workday. Around twelve, the noon whistle will sound, telling it is time to bridle the switch teams. On a good day, a team can be switched out in probably two minutes. Let's see NASCAR switch out two motors in less than two minutes, and they are using air tools. The driver will pull into the yard and circle around, pulling up to the man that is heading up the team. There is one person heading the team removing the neck yoke from the pole. There will be two barn people, one person on each side of the team, and the horses will be unhooked from the carriage. A person will take the lines from the driver, and the other person will hold the pole while the team is walked away and the pole is laid on the ground. While one is getting unhooked, the replacements are getting ready to be hooked up to the carriage. The horses are walked out to the carriage, then the person heading up the team will pull the horses around. The person that has the lines in his hands will give the lines to the driver. At this point, the other person will be lifting the pole so the horses can be backed onto it. The chains are hooked up, and the driver is on the way.

The hooking up of the teams and the switches is repeated over in the three-horse barn. All the barnmen and the farriers are involved. After switches, they will clean the barn again and feed those horses that came in for switches. At the end of the summer, the barnmen have a party, which is well deserved for all the work that they did throughout the summer. It is held the Sunday before Labor Day, the last day of switches, because of the change in the boat schedules.

Later, after the switches are done, the barnmen also have to go to the dock to get both round and square bales of hay, oats, and the Easy feed. The square bales have to be unloaded from the dray and put in the hayloft in the different barns. One barnman unloads the elevator and puts the bales on hand carts for the barnman wheeling the hay around the loft. Oats and Easy feed are unloaded and taken to the different barns by a forklift truck. This usually happens in the afternoon, until it is time for the carriages to come in for the day. The one man that makes sure that this work gets done is Dale Peterson. Also another man will be seen around the barn. He brings up the checks on payday and also lends a hand around the barn, usually around switch time. His name is Robert Gillespie. He has worked here for many years, and both of these people have taught me a thing or two about driving and backing a team of horses. Another person whose work is behind the scenes at the barn is Beau. This is the man who repairs the carriages when the brakes, poles, and tires go bad. When a carriage needs to be worked on, you will find Beau around the shop, working on a carriage. He also helps with getting carriages out in the morning, during switches, and when carriages are coming in for the day.

The work that the barnmen do is hard and repetitious; it is hard to describe all the things that these men do day in and day out, making sure things in the barnyard are going smoothly.

When I was on public tour, giving the downtown to Surrey Hill, a good friend of mine, Marvin Hubbard, and I would race to see who could be first out of the yard. It was only the two of us that were ready. We were at the barn so early we could have thrown the chickens out of the barn if there were any to be thrown out. Well, two years later, he did not come back to work. For a couple of years, there was no competition; it was not fun anymore. There was no one to try to beat. Then along came Tom Wright. We would become real good friends. He would come in and say, "I am going to beat Walter out of the barn today." He tried but was always second out. A couple of years later, he wanted to be the first person in the Mustang Bar for the grand opening. I arrived early and was sitting at the bar, watching Tom show up, and he was first in line. Just before the doors opened, I banged on the window to let Tom know that he was not going to be the first person in the Mustang for their grand opening.

One time it was time for hookup. I grabbed my holder and went to the two stalls where my team was supposed to be, but they were not there. Tom had moved my horses and put them in another empty stall. He got me good, and it was fun. Not to be outmaneuvered, two days later, while he was up in the locker room, getting ready, I was walking through the barn, collecting as many lead ropes as I could find, and then I tied each one behind his two horses. To get his horses out, each rope had to be individually untied. While he was with the company, it was not a job anymore. It was fun, and we had good memories.

Night Barn

As the day shift is coming to an arduous end, the night barn personnel are arriving. They are usually arriving around the time that the carriages are coming in for the day. They give the day barnmen a hand in putting the carriages away and unhooking the horses. After this is all done, each of the barnmen goes off to their respective barns to feed the horses in that barn for the evening. They will make sure the horses are pulling their hay, and they also fill the hay shoots and about every three hours thereafter.

When it comes to making sure the horses are pulling hay, for safety purposes, sometimes there will be two barnmen working together. If something happens to one person, the other can go for help. When I worked night barn, when I did not see someone for a while, I would check in on that person, making sure they were all right. Besides pulling hay and filling hay shoots, they are also cleaning the barns and making sure that all the horses are all right. Sometimes a horse will get a leg caught in a harness, and it will be the barnmen's job to unhook the harness and get the horse out of the harness. Sometimes a horse will intentionally put its foot in the harness so that someone will go to its aid, just like some horses will only eat the hay that is pulled for them. These are situations where the horse wants human contact and attention. I have seen horses turn their heads to see where the harness is and put their legs through the harness. We also have to deal with a horse that lies down and cannot get up.

With limited people, it is not fun at all; it is dangerous and very hard and tiring trying to get a large animal like a draft horse up. Cabs coming in for the end of the day also have to be dealt with, also the one or two switches for those that are covering the night shift. The night barnmen are not anywhere near as busy as the day barnmen are; with the limited personnel, they cannot be. The work has to be done, and it is necessary. It is arduous in that you have limited contact with people. If you are a people person, night barn is not the place for you.

When I first started at Carriage Tours, I was as a barnman. I could deal with the hard work. It was the harnessing of the horses that gave me the problem. If that task was not mastered, it would be a short career at Carriage Tours. One day, Dale Peterson approached me with a deal: I do night barn until he finds me a replacement, then I get to drive tours. Every morning, I would help Johnny Thompson harness his golf shuttle team. He had problems with his shoulder or arm, and so he showed me how to harness a team of horses. He would give me a ride halfway down the hill every morning. Every day I would go to bed at 0800 and wake up at noon because of the afternoon whistle. Four hours of sleep started to take their toll on me. I gave the company my two-week notice because of safety issues with my lack of sleep. The following day was my day off. I enjoyed it very much. I reported for work and was told that I had the night off and the next day off. They had found a replacement for me on night barn, and I would have my own tour buggy.

Johnny Thompson was responsible for helping me learn to harness a team of horses. Later on, he would also save my life when I was kicked in the chest by a horse. I had two broken ribs. The wind was knocked out of me. He and Marvin Hubbard pulled me out of the stall. When I went to the Mackinac Island Medical Center, the doctors were arguing whether or not I had a third broken rib. If I had a third, I was going to be transported to Petoskey for observation for twenty-four hours. It was going to be by helicopter. I was relieved when they said that, because there were rough seas in the Straits that day. No way was this cowboy getting on a boat that day. I had to see the doctor in four days. In those four days, I was bored out of my skull. I should have gone home to recover instead of asking the doctor to send me back to work, because the teams I had were not easy to drive. It bothered me some days worse than others. Now wet, cold days were bad rib days, and arthritis really bothered me on those days. They finally healed, but they would not heal correctly because when you breathe, your chest is moving in and out.

When heading to work, getting my horses ready for the day, I will meet a night barnman heading down the hill, giving him the greeting of the day, with the understanding that I have been there and done that.

THE FARRIERS

What is the difference between a blacksmith and a farrier?
Why are blacksmiths sometimes confused with farriers?
Name three different types of specialties in blacksmithing.

The drivers are responsible for combing and brushing their horses. They are also responsible for the washing and the harnessing of their horses, as well as making sure that all their horses have shoes on their feet before they leave the barn in the morning. When a horse or team is missing a shoe, the driver has to take the horse to see the farrier. The farriers are the men who shod the horses.

One of the farriers for our company is Keith Cripps; his dad was a jeweler in Toronto, where he engraved some of the names on the Stanley Cup. Keith is like an old country doctor while he is working; he likes to talk. His son Frank Cripps came up my first four years. Boy, was he good with the horses. He had a way with horses. What I mean is that there are certain horses that one farrier will have a problem with, but he managed to put shoes on the horse with no problem. Due to visa problems in 2009, Keith did not make it over that season. It was Eric Schuberg and Tom Horn. Eric, at one time, ran the Taxi Barn. One year in the off-season, Eric went to farrier school. In the 2009 season, it was him and Tom Horn shoeing the horses. A horse's hoof is made of a nerveless hornlike substance similar to the human fingernail, so being fitted for shoes affects the animal no more than a manicure affects people. Some horses like going to see the farrier, like some people like going to the dentist.

We have the Stone Age, then we have the Bronze Age, and then it was followed by the Iron Age. Iron was inferior to bronze for the early weapons. Iron is softer than bronze, spongy, and cannot hold an edge. The price is where iron is better. Bronze is by far the more expensive of the two. Iron can be alloyed with carbon to get steel. It is cheaper to field an army with iron weapons than with bronze. The Vikings, though, had a sword called the *VLFBERH+T*, or *ULFBERHT.* These swords were made of high-quality steel. The ingots of steel were acquired from the Volga trade route. The Volga trade route connected Northern Europe with Northwestern Russia by way of the Volga River. These swords were of high carbon content, very flexible, and were less brittle. It was the sword to have and was highly sought after, the same quality of steel you can get today. In battle they were the one to have and were highly sought after. The ingot of steel was placed in a crucible, not a forge. Temperatures in crucibles can get a lot hotter than with your typical forge. That is how they got their high-quality steel. Relics of antiquity seldom survived the Iron Age, because iron and steel readily oxidize and leave little trace.

As the Iron Age evolved, the term *blacksmithing* became associated with many different specialties. Sword smiths, also known as *bladesmith*, were the ones who made bladed weapons. They would make weapons such as knives, swords, daggers, and other bladed weapons. Armorers made the suits of armor. Locksmiths made the locks. Gunsmiths made the gun barrels and triggers. Farriers were the ones who shod the horses.

Horseshoeing and blacksmithing are two completely different things. Usually, the local blacksmith in a community is the man who has all these skills. Most horseshoers have limited knowledge of blacksmithing; it is limited to the fitting of horseshoes. There are plenty of smiths who never nailed or made a horseshoe. Sometimes you can find a horseshoer who is a good blacksmith, but in the smaller towns and country shops, the smith practices both trades out of necessity. This is probably how blacksmiths got associated with being the ones who shod the horses.

With approximately 360 heads of horses, these guys are probably the busiest. They prefer that the horses not be wet or muddy. If they are muddy, they appreciate it that you do not wash your horses before they are shod. They do not appreciate getting dripped on from the wet horse. Sometimes I have this bad habit of forgetting to check shoes before going to the wash rack—not a good thing to do. We usually have a long conversation about checking the horse's feet before going to the wash rack.

One time, one of my horses lost both of her hind shoes. Not thinking, I walked her through the dewy, wet grass. When we got to the farrier, he asked me why I washed my horse. Very defensively, I denied washing my horse, and then it dawned on me, and I explained that I had walked my horse through the dewy, wet grass instead of on the gravel driveway. When they were done with my horses, I always managed to thank them.

Some horses do not have a problem being shod, just like some people have no problem seeing a dentist. Some horses though do have a problem with visiting the farrier. I like to compare the horse's visit to see the farrier to our visit to the local dentist. I do not know of too many people who enjoy that visit to the local dentist, and most horses do not enjoy their visit to see the local farrier either. It is a necessary evil. It is necessary because the pavement that the horses are walking on day in and day out is like sandpaper on their hooves. The shoes are protecting the horses' feet. Sometimes while driving, if I would notice a loose shoe and if I knew the person well, as far as being around horses, I would ask if they could pull the shoe right off. The reason for this is because the loose shoe can injure the horse if they continue to walk on it. Sometimes during the day, while on the road, a shoe will come off. Depending on the time of day, if there is time for them to replace it and if it is the front or hind shoe, all these are taken into consideration in the decision to replace it now or wait until the following morning. If it is a front, they will make concerted effort to replace it right away.

Some of the horses wear a polyurethane shoe designed to absorb shock as they walk on pavement all day. Some are shod in steel all around. Regardless as to whether the horses wear the steel or the polyurethane shoe, that is a decision made by the farrier, and they will last anywhere from two to four weeks, depending on if the horses pick up their feet or if they drag their feet. The horses that stay the winter are usually shod in steel for traction on the ice and snow. The shoes that get worn out or are pulled off are thrown into a pile alongside the shop, which will be about five to six feet tall at the end of the season. They also shod some of the private horses on the island, including the Grand Hotel hitches.

They also help out in the yard, put hay up in the barns, help the driver unload the hay from the wagon, and help with the morning hookup and the switches in the afternoon. It is hard to explain or paint a picture of the work that is done. A lot has to be done in a short period. One time, it was late in the season. It was slow as all got out down at the ticket office that day, so slow that maybe two carriages went by, giving the tour all day. They had me in the yard instead of downtown for some reason. A load of hay came through the yard for Dray Barn. This was hay being brought over for the winter. Anyways, it was Jim Petit, Keith Cripps, Frank Cripps, and me. We all went to put hay up in Dray Barn. Jim Petit was on the wagon, and the rest of us were in the hay loft, stacking the hay as it came up the elevator. Keith and I would hand the hay up to Frank so he could stack it in the loft, ten bales high. It was getting to the point where we had to throw the bales up to Frank. There was a hole in the floor where you would come up the stairs into the loft. And that was one thing I had forgotten about. We were throwing the hay up to Frank. One time, I went to plant my foot to throw a bale of hay up to Frank, and that hole suddenly moved. My back foot never found the floor; it found the hole. There was this certain "Oh crap" look, and expletives came out of my mouth. Next thing I knew, I was falling down the stairs backward with the said bale of hay still in my hands. *Bump, bump, oh, good, we are done. Bump, bump, oh, we stopped. Bump, bump, bump, we are done. Nope. Bump, bump, we stopped. Here we go again. Bump, bump, bump, oh, good, the floor. Bam!* The head hit the floor and was busted open, bleeding like there was no tomorrow. Anyways, Jim Petit was going to take me down to the medical center, but before he could go, he wanted to see what work needed to be done up at Dray Barn for the winter.

Keith was getting mad at Petit, because the cut on my head was bleeding pretty good. They called me a cab to get me down to the med center. We got there in one piece, with Amanda driving; that was a given. For this driver, that was a privilege. They put about eight staples in my head. I did not feel a thing. They had to stay in for two to three weeks. Yikes, no haircut until the staples were out. No way was I getting a haircut until those stupid staples were out. My barber liked to apply pressure when he cut my hair. No, thank you. I will wait for the staples to come out before getting my haircut.

My hair was getting long and starting to bother me, mainly my ears. Well, I was able to survive two or three weeks with my hair long, tickling my ears. I got to my primary care doctor, signed in, waited about a half hour, got in the room, and anxiously waited for the doctor. He came in, starting with the small talk, wondering what happened. "What did you do to have those staples in your head?" All the staples came out but one,

Go figure. One had to go in crooked. I have a high pain threshold, but not this time. He had to numb the area around the staple, then he pulled the stupid thing out. Unfortunately, after my doctor visit, the barbershop was closed. Oh well, I waited this long for a haircut; one more day was not going to hurt.

THE KITCHEN

They say that an army runs on its stomach. The same can be said for Mackinac Island Carriage Tours. The ladies and, in this case, one man are the ones responsible for the feeding of the workers. We have breakfast, lunch, and dinner. Lunch is usually packed before or after breakfast and is eaten on the road by the drivers. Breakfast is probably the most important meal for me, because of the work that goes into getting my team ready. It usually consists of two eggs, two pieces of toast with honey, two pieces of sausages, potatoes, and oatmeal. While the eggs are cooking, I will be making my lunch. I will sometimes do a raid on the cookies. The best time to raid the cookies is at dinnertime; everybody is busy doing their own thing.

One time I had my cookies all wrapped and ready to go. One little problem—the head cook appeared to be watching me. This was a big problem. How was I going to get the cookies out? Then for two seconds, she turned her head. Like a flash, my hands swooped up the cookies and put them in my book bag, and I went back to my original position before she suspected anything. The rest of the kitchen was laughing because they had never seen me move so fast in my life.

Bologna and a piece of fruit will not cut it for lunch. It gets old after a while. Food is not to leave the kitchen. That is why the BLT is so coveted by this driver. Once a month, they serve bacon for breakfast, and then I make my BLT. I will casually make my toast and then go to the counter and put the mayonnaise, lettuce, and tomato on my toast. I will take it back to my place and then get my breakfast, putting the bacon on my sandwich and tucking it away in my lunch bag as though nothing happened. Breakfast sandwiches also do a good job of filling the order as well as of taking care of the palate. Kevin, the morning cook, will give me a piece of fruit for the day and remind me that my eggs are done.

Breakfast is usually a quiet time for me. Every once in a while, Ernie will come down for breakfast and, for whatever reason, try to get me going, pushing all the buttons he knows to get me riled. Most of the time, it works. Ernie likes to talk in the morning, and I am the quiet one. Once I get to the barn, I would go over and see Ernie and have a morning talk with him before we both are on the road. In the end, it was all in fun. Later in the day, I will be waiting in line for the ticket office, sometimes in the rain, laughing at what went on earlier in the morning. While everybody is out working, dinner is being prepared.

I usually look forward to dinner; by midafternoon, I am ready for dinner. It is the one time during the day that I can have a chance to unwind from the long day that I just went through. I am pretty much unwound to begin with, because I usually walk to and from work every day. Most of the other employees will race down the hill on their bikes. While walking down the hill from work, everything that went on at work during the day is left at the top of the hill. I like the walk because it allows me to sort things out in my mind. Sometimes I will stop at Trinity Church at the bottom of Fort Hill and reflect on things that are going on in my life. It is nice to just sit there and hear nothing but you and the faint sounds going on outside. Then I will head for Lennox for dinner.

I am glad to have a conversation, and having a two-way conversation during dinner makes me feel good. Sometimes you need a release. When I am driving the front half of the tour, it is one of the few times during the day I can have a conversation with another person. The whole day, for ten to thirteen trips, I am doing all the talking. I am ready to have a two-way conversation with someone else. I get tired of hearing myself talk. This is where I will also get any mail that is sent to me, usually in the form of bills and sometimes letters from home. I will then have my dinner, talk to some of my friends, confiscate anything snacky for my lunch, and thank the ladies for the wonderful dinner.

They are more than just cooks; I typically hung out with them after dinner. They wash my white livery shirts and my pants. Two of those people were Brenda Topam and Mac Armstrong. They were from Meaford, Ontario. They were real good friends that I typically hung out with after dinner. He was a plow truck driver for the province of Ontario in the off-season. Brenda worked in her son's grocery store. Crown Royal and Diet Coke were her drinks. They, Mac and Brenda, would also bring me back those maple leaf cookies with maple-flavored cream on the inside. Oh boy, are they ever good. There are those chocolate-covered ones that are just as sinful. They are also there to listen when I need to talk to someone. There are people here who are younger than I am. There are also some who are older than I am, but not too many that are of my age. I will usually gravitate toward the older crowd. What I am trying to say is that it is those small things that make life bearable that matters the most to me. Moments like these are important to me, and that makes them worth more than their weight in gold.

THE KINGS OF THE ISLAND (THE HORSE)

Why are horses so important on Mackinac Island?
What happens to the horses at the end of the tourist season?
Approximately how many horses are on Mackinac
Island during the summertime?

During the summer, Mackinac Island has around 450 to 500 horses on the island. Out of the approximately 500 horses, around 286 of those are owned by Mackinac Island Carriage Tours. It is the world's largest livery and carriage operation. The three main breeds that the company works with are Clydesdales, Belgians, and Percheron, both dapple-gray and black. On the teams, there are no stallions. Both geldings and mares are working for the company on the teams. The company has geldings working together and mares working together, and they have mares and geldings teamed together. *Draft* means "to pull"; that is how we get draft horses. Also the bartender has to pull a lever or handle to get you that cold draft beer. The draft horses were the engines that helped build this country. Later on, when they were going out of style, like the landline is today, most believed they would never come back, but they did in a big way. Ninety-five percent of all heavy draft horses are either Belgian, coming from Belgium, or Percheron, coming from France.

Belgian. Throughout the Middle Ages, it was known as the Flanders horse (after the region in Europe from which it originated) and had great influence on the development of other draft horse breeds, such as the Suffolk punch, the Clydesdale, and the Shire. Throughout the centuries, Belgian breeders resisted pressure to produce lighter cavalry horses and concentrated on breeding the Brabant, or the Belgian heavy draft, which was well suited to the climate and rich, heavy soil of the region.

The Belgians of North America are divided into two groups, modern and old style. Modern, or American, Belgians are leggier and have more slope to the shoulder than the old-style Belgians, or the Brabant. In the United States, the former are common while the latter are relatively rare. The Belgian has been bred for its ability to efficiently convert feed to flesh and muscle. This horse has heavy muscling, a deep chest, wide barrel, powerful hind quarters, and an active boldness yet is willing and docile. These traits have made the Belgian the most popular draft horse in the United States among horse farmers, loggers, and pullers. Color: American—sorrel, roan, chestnut; Brabant—roan or bay. Mature weight, 1,400–1,800; mature height, 16–17 hands. One hand is about four inches.

Percheron. The Percheron is probably from the Perche province of France, from which the horse gets its name. There are a number of theories as to where the horses came from. No matter the theory of origin, breed historians agree that the terrain and climate of the Perche area had the greatest influence on the development of the breed. During the seventeenth century, horses from Perche, the ancestors of the current Percheron, were smaller, standing between fifteen and sixteen hands tall, and more agile. These horses were almost uniformly gray in color. Paintings and drawings from the Middle Ages generally show French knights on mounts of this color. After the days of the armored knight, the emphasis in horse breeding was shifted so as to develop horses better able to pull heavy stage coaches at a fast trot. Gray horses were preferred because their light coloring was more visible at night. This new type of horse was called the diligence horse, because the coach they pulled was named diligences. After the stagecoach was replaced by rail, the modern Percheron type arose as a slightly heavier horse for use in agriculture and heavy-hauling work, moving goods from docks to railway terminals. Between 1789 and the 1800s, the Percheron was in danger of becoming extinct as horse breeding was suppressed during the French Revolution and its aftermath. Some of characteristics of the Percheron are as follows: They are compact and muscular yet retain their Arabian ancestry and elegance. The neck is crested, and the face is refined with large dark eyes. The Percheron have little feathering on the legs. Colors are black, blue, roan, and dapple-gray; in some areas, they prefer sorrel. Characteristically, the Percheron are either black or gray in color (gray horses are born black and dapple out over time until they become pure white, usually by age twelve). The average mature weight is 1,500 pounds. The temperament of these beautiful animals is as follows: active, energetic, good-natured, and intelligent. The use for these animals is as follows: heavy draft, driving, carriage service, riding.

Clydesdale. When you talk about draft horses, somewhere along the way, the subject of the Clydesdale will pop up like clockwork on my tour. On every tour that I gave, the most popular question would have to be, Are there any Clydesdales on the island? When I was a tour driver, there were no Clydesdales on the island, but now the company owns a pair of Clydesdales. Clydesdales originated in the Clyde River Valley of Scotland. Abundant white feathering on the feet is a trademark of this breed, although those who work horses in the field find the extra grooming to keep the feathering clean to be a slight detriment. Clydesdale is therefore commonly seen in exhibition hitches for brewery companies and in shows and parades. Clydesdales are usually bay in color, but roan, black, gray, and chestnut also occur. Most have white markings, including white on the face, feet, legs, and occasional body spotting (generally the lower belly). They also have extensive feathering on their lower legs. The conformation of the Clydesdale has changed significantly throughout its history. In the 1920s and 1930s, it was a compact horse smaller than the Shire, Percheron, and Belgian. Beginning in the 1940s, breeding animals were selected to produce taller horses that looked more impressive in parades and shows. Today, the Clydesdale stands sixteen to eighteen hands (64 to 72 inches, 163 to 183 cm) high and weighs 1,800 to 2,000 pounds. The breed has a straight or slightly convex facial profile, broad forehead, and wide muzzle. It is well-muscled and strong, with an arched neck, high withers, and a sloped shoulder.

When talking about Clydesdales, somewhere along the line while talking about the draft horse, the Budweiser hitch will come up. Speaking of those beautiful guys, here are some interesting history and facts of one of the more popular hitches. Here is a look into the colorful history of the Budweiser Clydesdale hitch. On April 7, 1933, August A. Busch and Adolphus Busch III surprised their father, August A. Busch Sr. with the gift of a six-horse Clydesdale hitch to commemorate the repeal of Prohibition. The Clydesdales made a stop in Washington, DC, in April 1933 to reenact the delivery of one of the first cases of Budweiser to Pres. Franklin Delano Roosevelt. The actual delivery had been shipped by air and presented on April 7, 1933. Shortly after the hitch was introduced, the six-horse Clydesdale team was increased to eight. On March 30, 1950, in commemoration of the opening of the Newark Brewery, a Dalmatian was introduced as the Budweiser Clydesdales' mascot.

Hitch requirements. In order for one of Budweiser Clydesdale horses to qualify for one of the traveling hitches, it must be a gelding, four years of age, stand seventy-two inches at the shoulder when fully mature, weigh between 1,800 to 2,300 pounds, have a bay coat, four white legs, a white blaze, and a black mane and tail.

Feed. Each hitch horse will consume as much as twenty to twenty-five quarts of whole grains, minerals, and vitamins; fifty to sixty pounds of hay; and thirty gallons of water per day.

Hitch locations. There are five traveling Budweiser Clydesdale hitches; they are based in Saint Louis, Missouri; Menifee, California; Merrimack, New Hampshire; and San Antonio, Texas. The Budweiser Clydesdales can be viewed at the Anheuser-Busch breweries in Saint Louis, Merrimack, and Fort Collins, Colorado. The Budweiser Clydesdales may be viewed at Grant's Farm, the 281-acre ancestral home of the Busch family in Saint Louis, Missouri, and the following Anheuser-Busch theme parks: Busch Gardens in Williamsburg, Virginia, and Tampa, Florida, and at the

SeaWorld theme parks in Orlando, Florida; San Diego, California; and San Antonio, Texas.

Handlers. Expert grooms travel on the road with the hitch. They are on the road at least ten months every year. When necessary, one handler has night duty to provide round-the-clock care for the horses, ensuring their safety and comfort.

Transport. Ten horses, the famous red, white, and gold beer wagon, and other essential equipment are transported in three fifty-foot tractor trailers. Cameras in the trailers (with monitors in the cabs) enable the drivers to keep a watchful eye on their precious cargo during transport. The team stops each night at local stables, so the "gentle giants" can rest. Air-cushion suspension and thick rubber flooring in the trailers ease the rigors of traveling.

Drivers. Driving the twelve tons of wagon and horses requires quite a bit of strength and skill. The forty pounds of reins the driver holds, plus the tension of the reins equals seventy-five pounds. All hitch drivers are put through rigorous training period before they are given the reins.

Harness. Each harness and collar weighs approximately 130 pounds. The harness is handcrafted with solid brass and patent leather and stitched with pure linen thread. The harness is made to fit any Clydesdale; however, collars come in various sizes and must be individually fitted to the Clydesdale, like a finely tailored suit.

Horseshoes. Their horseshoes measure twenty inches from end to end and weigh about five pounds, which is more than twice as long and about five times as heavy as the shoe worn by a light pleasure horse. As I said before, a horse's hoof is made of a nerveless horn-like substance similar to the human fingernail, so being fitted for shoes affects the animal no more than a manicure affects people.

Wagons. Turn-of-the-century beer wagons have been meticulously restored and are kept in excellent repair. The wagons are equipped with two braking systems: a hydraulic pedal device that slows the vehicle for turns and downhill descents and a hand brake that locks the rear wheels when the wagon is at a halt.

Dalmatians. The Dalmatian breed has been traveling with the Clydesdale hitch since the 1950s. The Dalmatian has long been associated with horses and valued for their speed, endurance, and dependable nature. Dalmatians were known as coach dogs because they ran between the wheels of coaches and carriages and were companions to the horses. Dalmatians were historically used by brewers to guard the wagon while the driver was making deliveries. Today, the Dalmatian is perched atop the wagon, proudly seated next to the driver.

There are also privately owned pleasure horses on Mackinac Island. Between the draft horses and the pleasure horses, at peak of season between Memorial Day and Labor Day, there are about 450 to 500 heads of horses on the island. There are two large animal veterinarians (DVM). There is one doctor on the island. Two vets and one doctor—you tell me who runs the island. Dr. Bill Chambers is also one of the owners of Mackinac Island Carriage Tours. He takes care of the small animals on the island as well. The other vet was Dr. Allan Sibinic. He had a special gift. As part of his practice when he lived in Charlevoix, he took care of both large and small animals, which worked out well for the island.

With all the horses and the manure that comes with the horse, you have flies. The island in the past couple of years has done a real good job at keeping the flies under control. They do not use chemical sprays; instead they use fly predators from Spalding. Fly predators spend their life cycle in and around manure piles and other decaying material. Because they spend their life cycle in and around manure piles and other decaying matter, they will not become pests. The fly predators eat the pupa of the flies. With the predator flies and some other practices, such as keeping the streets clean by picking up the manure during the day and flushing the streets at night, the island has really done a good job at getting the pesky flies under control. Also, the street sweepers clean up the manure that the horses leave as a calling card. Of all the jobs on Mackinac Island, keeping the manure off the streets goes a long way in fly control and prevention of other health issues as well. With the fly predators, you are targeting a specific group of insects. With chemical sprays, you indiscriminately kill all insects, and some of those are good. The island also has some American brown bats. They are currently having a problem with white nose syndrome. It is Mackinac Island's form of mosquito control. One bat in one night can eat twice its weight in mosquitoes. Someone figured it out to be around 1,800 mosquitoes for one bat per night. That someone was paid a lot of money to figure that out, and obviously it was not me.

The Grand Hotel guests have been treated with elegance since 1887. Visitors today get the same treatment as if they were in the Victorian age. Upon arrival from the ferry, a large maroon bus with a red-coated driver in top hat and a dappled-gray team or black team of Percheron take the guests up to the Grand Hill to their accommodations. Up by Surrey Hill, there is a barn that is the stables for the Grand Hotel and Mackinac Island Carriage Tours. It is also the museum for carriages as well. The barn houses a very unique collection of early twentieth-century carriages, many of which are still in use today. Carriages range in size from a small opera bus to a basket vis-à-vis with woven cane seat sides and fenders, made by C. P. Kimball & Co. of Chicago. The English name for this popular coachman-driven summer carriage was "sociable." Another carriage in the Grand Hotel collection is a Stanhope gig made by Brewster & Co. of New York. A four-passenger trap made by Studebaker Brothers of Chicago is included in the collection, along with several wagons, omnibuses, a surrey, and sleighs and cutters for winter use. They lease their Percheron teams from Mackinac Island Carriage Tours. The Percheron teams are usually black or dapple-gray. The Grand Hotel also has two teams of Hackneys, which they own. Ben Mosley is currently the stable master for the Grand Hotel.

The island is all things horse—draft horse, pleasure horse, even little horses. The pleasure horse can also be used for driving as well. Throughout the season, one of the vets one or two nights a week talks to a tour group about the horses that work and live part of their lives on the island. The island is a continual "celebration of the horse and all things horse."

The Festival of the Horse brings many educational and fun horse-related things. With the festival, they have a driving competition, a parade, and a lot of other things involving the horse. The Lilac Festival has a parade that includes "a lot of outside" horses of all breeds, including Belgian, Percheron, Haflingers, Clydesdales, Hackneys, and an assortment of pleasure horses. Down at Little Barn, which is over in the Mission District, we have the little ponies for the youngsters to start out on. It is a real good introduction to the horse for the youngsters.

I had some horse background before I started working for carriage tours. I knew that all big horses were not Clydesdales. For a lot of people, they automatically think of all big draft horses as Clydesdales. At the same time, when you point out to them distinct differences between the different breeds, it is nice to see the green light go on. "Oh, I see now. Okay, I get it." That is when I know I have done my job right. We sure do love it when the Budweiser Clydesdale hitch gets to come over and show off for us. It is way bigger than a three-ring circus coming to town for us horse lovers! The Budweiser Clydesdale hitch also has its own following. It is a beautiful treat when you do get to see those magnificent guys.

LILACS AND THE LILAC FESTIVAL

Are lilacs native to Mackinac Island?
How many different varieties of lilac are there?
About how many different colors of lilac are there?

When you first arrive on Mackinac Island, you will first notice that the air is not filled with exhaust fumes from automobiles. It is fresh, and depending on what time of the year you arrive, you may even smell lilac around the first week in June or whenever the lilac decides to start to bloom. The blooming of the lilac depends on the weather that we have in the spring. They are always hoping for the lilac to bloom in time for Lilac Festival, held the week before Father's Day in June. During the Lilac

Festival, the island holds a photography contest to see who can take the best photograph of the lilac on the island. The Lilac Parade is usually held on Father's Day, bringing a beautiful end to the festival. Henry David Thoreau probably was the first person to write about the lilacs on Mackinac Island. He only listed them once. He recognized also that lilacs are propagated by humans, not by animals or blown seeds. And when people were gone, they were an indicator that someone had once lived there.

The origins of the lilac lay in the mountains of Asia, more than likely in the Balkans. They were hybridized over in France. Lilacs migrated to this country during precolonial and colonial times. They were taken from their native habitat and moved to France and England to add flavor to their gardens. They are the plant's true roots, having brought with them unique and newly hybridized French lilacs.

They are probably the largest but not necessarily the oldest. In 2007, the International Lilac Society went around the island to determine the age of some of the trees. With permission from the property owners who appeared to own the largest lilacs, they took small bore samples from the trunks. Wounds would heal within a year. By counting the rings and some calculations, they could determine the age of that particular trunk. The test confirmed that the oldest lilacs tested were no older than 130–140 years old. That placed them in the range of being planted between 1870 and 1880. These were wealthy people who wanted a plant they could highlight in their fabulous gardens. They paid a lot of money for these lilacs so they could own a plant that no one else could have. Some went as far as hiring a plant hunter. These guys got paid a lot of money to do nothing more than traverse the world, hunting down rare species of plants. Ernest Henry Wilson and George Forrest are just a couple of these plant hunters. For people who like lilac, Mackinac Island is a mecca.

The care for these plants is that they need plenty of sunlight, trimming away of the suckers, and trimming away all the dead branches. These take away energy and moisture that the plant can use elsewhere. There is probably between one thousand and two thousand lilacs on the island. There are 250 in public places, 180 alone are in Marquette Park. There are about one hundred different varieties and around eighteen variations in color. Some lilacs are twenty-six to twenty-seven inches in diameter and are thirty to forty feet tall and between 130 and 150 years old.

They also have a collection of rare lilac up around Surrey Hill. These lilacs were located down by the harbor. And when the state of Michigan did some renovations to the harbor, the lilacs were not part of the plans. They were rescued by Mary McGwire, and Dr. Bill Chambers had a Dray take them up to Surrey Hill. There they were planted and cared for. It took them a while to recover from all the stress, but they have recovered remarkably well.

The lilac is not native to Mackinac Island. In the 1800s following the Civil War, Mackinac Island became a popular resort destination for the wealthy. Mackinac Island has the temperate climate that attracts the visitors and also makes it great for lilacs to grow. For the same reasons, it is great for growing lilac. It is the reason the wealthy frolicked around on Mackinac Island.

LILAC QUEENS OF THE PAST

In 1947, Stella King, who was a nurse on the island, and Dr. Bill Chambers, who was a large-animal veterinarian on the island, talked about having a lilac festival. They wanted to celebrate spring. Initially, the festival was a weekend-long event. Now it lasts for a full ten days. In 1949, when the Lilac Festival first began, the police booth was where the taxi stand is today. They used to post photographs of the Lilac Queen candidates, and the public selected the winner. Today the candidates are nominated and selected by their high school classmates.

Past Lilac Queens are the following: 1949, Sue Perault; 1950, Mary Dennany; 1951, Jeanie Vance; 1952, Catherine McGreevy; 1953, Joann Goodheart; 1954, Linda Horn; 1955, unknown; 1956, Judy Dufina; 1957, Alice Bunker; 1958, Sandra Gallagher; 1959, Anna Joyce Andress;

1960, Sharon Schmidt; 1961, Joann Sawyer; 1962, Beverly Brown; 1963, Margaret Doud; 1964, Nancy Chambers; 1965, Nancy Pfeiffelman and Cindy Francis; 1966, Melly Alford; 1967, Loretta Cowell; 1968, Cathy Cowell; 1969, Deborah Rogers; 1970, Deborah DeLavern; 1971, Dorothy Gillespie; 1972, Patty Trayser; 1973, Amanda St. Onge; 1974, Cindy Cadotte; 1975, Barbara Gillespie; 1976, Ellen Putnam; 1977, Martha Bodwin; 1978, Joyce Olson; 1979, Midge Bodwin; 1980, Anna Rogers; 1981, Margaret Gallagher; 1982, Carol Ouellette; 1983, Velma LaPine; 1984, Tonya Bazinau; 1985, Tammy LaPine; 1986, Louann Kolatski; 1987, Michelle McLean; 1988, Doris Bradley; 1989, Katrina Platzke; 1990, Vanessa Smith; 1991, Heather Chambers; 1992, Mariah Horn; 1993, Lisa Doud; 1994, Tawna Urman; 1995, Erica Jones; 1996, Peggy Bynoe; 1997, Jennifer Putnam; 1998, Heather Campagnola; 1999, Christine Ball; 2000, Tracy Quinter; 2001, Polly Smith; 2002, Roxanne Pettit; 2003, Sara Wessel; 2004, Jennifer Wightman; 2005, Blisse Beardsley; 2006, Melissa Bunker; 2007, Kristi Kamphuis; 2008, Jane Finkel; 2009, Michi Mullings; 2010, Marie Bunker; 2011, Adrienne Rilenge; 2012, Zhane Nash.

SAINTE ANNE'S CHURCH

Why were the British concerned about a Catholic Church?
When there was no priest available, who conducted Mass?
For how long did they go without a priest?
How many times was the church moved?

The sainted priest Ignatius Loyola, commander in chief of the army of Spain in 1521, was severely wounded in battle and made a vow that should he recover, he would devote his life to God. He was the founder of the historic Society of Jesus, the famed order of the Jesuits. The ancient painting of Saint Ignatius Loyola may be freely viewed by visitors at the Saint Ignace Church. Sainte Anne's is probably the oldest Catholic congregation dedicated to Sainte Anne in North America; they have baptismal records dating back to April 1695. Sainte Anne's Catholic Church was established as a mission first by Father Claude Dablon, a Jesuit missionary, as he wintered on Mackinac Island in 1670–1671. The following year, in the spring of 1671, Father Jacques Marquette established the mission across the Straits where Saint Ignace is presently located. He needed a safe refuge for the converted Christians under Father Marquette's immediate care from the pagans. The First Nations were Huron; the threat were other members of Huron tribe who did not convert. The Huron's home range was the western part of Ontario, so Father Marquette wanted Lake Huron between him and the threat. In 1708, the Odawa and their Jesuit priests moved to the south shore of the Straits of Mackinac (today Mackinaw City.) On May 17, 1673, Father Marquette and French explorer Louis Jolliet left Saint Ignace and explored the upper regions of the Mississippi. They went as far south as the Arkansas River, arriving there on July 17,1673. That is close to 1,400 miles. They returned to the region two years later where Father Marquette got ill and died on May 18, 1675. He was temporally buried somewhere by the Pere Marquette River over Ludington. A year later, the remains were recovered and taken back to Saint Ignace, where he is permanently buried. If it were not for all the missionaries like Father Marquette and Louis Jolliet, we would not have a documented history of this period. They were required to keep track of everything they encountered and saw. The diaries, when filled, were then sent to Quebec, Canada, and then to France. There is a repository at the university in Quebec where these diaries may be read.

In 1744, the French established a congregation and built a church and named it Sainte Anne's. She was the patron saint of the voyageurs and fur traders. In 1761, the British won the Seven Years' War, or the French and Indian War, receiving all the holdings of the French in North America east of the Mississippi River. The French settlers were allowed to stay as long as they signed their allegiance to the king of England. The settlers continued to practice their religion as best as they could without a priest. The missionary was recalled in 1765. They would not have a resident priest again until 1830 when Father Mazzuchelli arrived. It survived sixty-five years without a priest. They practiced privately in their homes. For the baptisms, the post commandant was to perform and record. Every once in a while, a priest would come by and have regular Mass and consecrate hosts. Parish leaders cared for the church and the priest's house. In the winter of 1780 and 1781, the British moved the community to the safety of Mackinac Island during the American Revolution. The British lieutenant governor Patrick Sinclair ordered the dismantling of Sainte Anne's, hoping to encourage the French Canadians to follow the British to Mackinac Island. The log church was rebuilt along the shores of the island's protected bay below the cliffs where later will be the location of the fort. The church was located near the site where the Village Inn is now located.

The cemetery was located around where the Twilight and Windsor are now located. In 1924, most of the graves were disinterred and moved to the center of the island, where it is now located. All this time, the congregation is still looking for a permanent priest. What makes the moving of the church so remarkable is that the Catholic Church did away with the British. The Catholic Church was fed up with the divorces of King Henry VIII. You have to ask yourself, why were the British so concerned about a Catholic Church? You have to look at who was keeping the fort running—the storekeepers, the blacksmiths, the farriers, and anyone else that made the running of the fort possible. The answer is the French—there would be no one to run the fort if it were not for the French.

The steadfast dedication of the parishioners was what sustained the parish through the difficult times. Magdelaine LaFramboise and her husband were prominent fur traders on the island at that time. After he was murdered, she took over the business. Later she procured a license and took up permanent residence on Mackinac Island. They were one of the most successful fur traders in Western Michigan. She was of mixed Odawa and French blood. She knew four different languages. She also was godmother to many baptisms and witness to many marriages. She was a host to many prominent visitors who came to the island. She provided leadership through the first half of the nineteenth century for the Catholic community on Mackinac Island. She donated the property adjacent to her home when the leaders decided to move the church and priest's house to the current site on the east side of the harbor in the mid-1820s. In exchange for the gift of land, LaFramboise asked to be buried beneath the altar at the end of her life. LaFramboise died on April 4, 1846. Father Henri Van Renterghem of Sainte Anne's honored the request of Magdelaine LaFramboise and had her interred beneath the altar of the church. In the

1960s, Sainte Anne's was renovated, and a basement and activity center were added. The remains of LaFramboise, as well as those of her daughter Josephine Pierce and her infant daughter Josette, who had been buried with her, were relocated and interred in Sainte Anne's churchyard. In 1984, she was elected into the state's Women's Hall of Fame. A historic marker marks the spot and also recognizes LaFramboise and her contributions. In 2013, Sainte Anne's built a crypt in the church for re-interment of the remains of Magdelaine LaFramboise, and two of her relatives were placed in the crypt. When the remains were re-interred, some of her family and some of her descendants were present. She is now at rest, back where she belongs in the church, in the museum in the basement of the church.

In the 1870s, the little log church that had survived two moves was torn down and replaced with an imposing Gothic structure. In the 1890s, parish leaders, along with Father Antoine Rezek, decided to do a major restoration and redecoration. He would leave in 1891 with the knowledge that the restoration project was fully funded. The appearance of the church after the restoration would carry it through the twentieth century. A hundred years later, in the 1990s, the church was once again in need of restoration, recapturing the 1890s appearance. In the 1930s, 1940s, 1950s, and 1960s, there were some facelifts. In the 1960s was when they started to dig the basement for the church. That was when they found Magdelaine LaFramboise. Along came Pope John Paul XXIII with the Second Vatican Council. The stand-alone table was removed, along with the statues and the confessional. In 1997, the church went under a restoration, with the permission from the bishop that Sainte Anne's could keep its historical appearance. In true Renaissance fashion, a new mural depicting Sainte Anne, Mary, and the baby Jesus with a view of Mackinac Island in the distance was created for the church. It is everything as beautiful as the Sistine Chapel done by Michelangelo. In the winter of 2011, the stained glass windows were cleaned, the lead seals were repaired, and in some areas where the glass was cracked, they were replaced at a cost of about $200,000.

Sainte Anne's has three different congregations; you have the islanders, the tourists, and the workers. They have Spanish Mass for the Mexican workers on Tuesday nights and Jamaican Mass on Wednesday nights, and on Thursdays, they have a supper or dinner where the food is donated by establishments from the island, and they also have a Filipino Mass on Thursday evenings. They hold square dances on Tuesday evenings, where all three congregations have a chance to meet. Mackinac Island has about 450 to 500 permanent residents; approximately one hundred of those are Catholic. The church, in order to stay running throughout the winter, is dependent upon the summer visitors and some of the employees to get it through the winter. In the winter, they hold Mass in the basement, because it costs a lot to heat the church.

The Jesuits still have a presence on the island today. The Jesuits still run it as a mission as they did over three hundred years ago. It has survived sixty-five years without a resident priest. The steadfast dedication of the parish is what has sustained it through the difficult times. Every year, in September, there is a pilgrimage from Dearborn, Michigan, to Mackinac Island. The Chaldeans come to Mackinac Island for the celebration of the Feast of the Holy Cross. It is usually in the early fall, usually in September. They speak the beautiful language that Jesus Christ our Lord spoke.

There are three other churches on the island, and they are the Little Stone Church, Trinity Church, and Mission Church. All the churches on the island hold weddings during the summer months. The Little Stone Church is probably the number one church on the island for weddings. The summer of 2007, there were around thirty-nine weddings held at Little Stone Church. Proceeds from the weddings go to a scholarship fund for island students. There is no waiting list for weddings. It is Union Congregational, built all of fieldstone found here on the island, and completed in 1913. Windows were hand painted and donated, depicting scenes from the island's history by Elizabeth Hubbard, daughter of Gurdon Hubbard, who purchased the property in the Annex. They have a regular Sunday Mass during the tourist season.

The other church that is just as quaint as the Little Church is Trinity Church. It was originally painted brown and green to represent the Little Brown Church in the Vale. For years, if you wanted an Episcopal Church service, people would go to the post chapel at Fort Mackinac, and sometimes they were held at the courthouse. The church was built in 1873. The soldiers at the fort built the two chancel chairs. This is the church that, for the past five years, I and some other island employees get together and hold hymn singing. Just bring your voice. Some hymns that we will sing are "The Little Brown Church in the Vale," "Power in the Blood," "In the Garden," "I'll Fly Away," and "A Closer Walk with Thee," just to name a few. They have a regular Sunday Mass during the tourist season. In the winter, Mass is held in the parsonage. Sometimes at the end of the day, on my way home from work, if it is open when I am passing by, I will stop there and sit down, just think things over for a bit and unload and enjoy the serenity.

The last church that I will talk about is the Mission Church. This is probably Michigan's oldest Presbyterian Church, established in 1837 by William Ferry. It was built of the old Colonial style of architecture. The church was also a boarding school on the island for Indian and Métis children. This is where influence from Magdelaine LaFramboise helped William Ferry. The church is now a museum. One can hold a wedding in any of these four churches from the end of April to the end of October.

ROUND ISLAND LIGHTHOUSE

How many lighthouses are in the state of Michigan?
About how many lighthouses are still operational?
How many different shapes were lighthouses built in Michigan?
What shape is similar to Round Island Lighthouse?

Before I worked on Mackinac Island as a tour driver, as a youngster I really had no appreciation for the maritime history of the Great Lakes. Where I lived, we were landlocked. Hemlock is about eighteen miles west of Saginaw, Michigan. The only appreciation came from the wreck of the *Edmund Fitzgerald*. When the gales of November came early on November 10, 1975, the 729-foot long ore carrier *Edmund Fitzgerald* went down in thirty-five-foot seas on Lake Superior, and ninety-eight miles per hour gusts of winds were recorded at Whitefish Point Lighthouse that night. That is equivalent to a category 2 hurricane. I was in sixth grade at that time and had questions. To this day, no straight answers as to why the largest ore carrier on the Great Lakes at that time sank. Only a lot of speculation and conjecture surround the wreck. For some reason, I became interested in the maritime history of the Great Lakes. There are no answers today as to why and how the largest ore carrier sank. The only ones that know what happened that night on Lake Superior are the twenty-nine crew members of the *Edmund Fitzgerald*, and they are forever in our memories, under 550 feet of water, at the bottom of Lake Superior. They say the bell is the soul of the ship, and each one has a different tune. The bell represents the voice of the ship, the voices of those who went down with her. The bell from the *Edmund Fitzgerald* has been removed and is on display in the maritime museum at Whitefish Point, replaced with a brass bell. Engraved are the names of all crewmembers, and it was placed on the deck of the ship. This is the beginning of my interest in the maritime history of the Great Lakes and the lighthouses that guide the ships through the precarious passages. Lighthouses are beacons that help guide ships through hazardous waters.

Michigan has the largest coastline in the United States, with about 3,200 miles, and to go along with that distinction, we have the most lighthouses at 124. Sixty-four of these are still operational today. Point Betsie Lighthouse and Sherwood Point Lighthouse were the last manned lighthouses on the Great Lakes in the United States in the fall of 1983; in 1998, Boston Harbor Lighthouse was the last manned lighthouse in the United States, manned today just for token purposes.

Round tower lighthouses are typically built of brick and may or may not be encased in a steel shell for protection. They may be large or small. Skeletal lighthouses are those that use a steel skeleton framework to support the light on top. Only a few are constructed of wood. Conical lighthouses can be classified similar to round lighthouses. If the light tower gets narrower at the top, then you can classify it as conical. Square/integral lighthouses are one with the tower built into the house and are square in design. An example of this will be Round Island Lighthouse in Lake Huron. Schoolhouse lighthouses were constructed similar to an old schoolhouse, thus the name. This was a common style.

04/10/2010

One of the main characters for the building of lighthouses on the Upper Great Lake is Orlando M. Poe. His title was army engineer of the Upper Lakes Lighthouse District. His district was enormous, featuring eighty-two active lighthouses and beacons. He was also responsible for the maintenance of existing lighthouses and construction of new facilities. His job title was engineer secretary for the lighthouse board. After that, he was promoted to chief army engineer of the Upper Lakes Lighthouse District. He was responsible for the Detroit River, Lake Saint Clair, and Lakes Huron Superior and Michigan. He was also responsible for various harbor and river projects in Eastern Michigan, as well as the Saint Mary's River in the Upper Peninsula.

The district was immense, featuring eighty-two active lighthouses and lighted beacons. He was also supposed to issue annual reports with recommendations for locations for new lighthouses. Spectacle Reef was the lighthouse on his to-do list and was a most intimidating project. Its distinguishing feature is the two rocky projections seven feet below the surface of the water. It is located ten miles from Bois Blanc Island and seventeen miles from the mainland. This will be the most expensive lighthouse in US history, at $400,000. Weather conditions on Lake Huron played a role in the cost. Other lighthouses that he built were the New Presque Isle Lighthouse between Alpena and Rogers City, South Manitou Island Lighthouse, Grosse Point Lighthouse, Outer Island Lighthouse, Au Sable Lighthouse located at opposite ends of Lake Superior, Little Sable Point, and Seul Choix [sis-shwa] Point Lighthouse.

The lighthouses that he designed were tall brick structures, gently tapering from top to bottom, displaying an embellished array of masonry gallery supports and arched top windows. This unique mix soon came to be known as the Poe style. What was then the largest shipping lock in the world at Sault Saint Marie, Michigan, was also his duty to design and build.

It would be known as the Poe Lock. He did not live long enough to see the completion of the Lock. Poe passed away at the age of sixty-three, in his Detroit home. All the beacons that he built are all still standing today. Southwest of Spectacle Reef Lighthouse is the site of Orlando Poe's crowning achievement in lighthouse design, the Poe Reef. It lies eight feet below the surface of the water. It was once marked by four different lightships in 1929. A lighthouse was built on top of it, a twenty-five-foot square, three-story building topped by a smaller square fourth story, sitting on a sixty-four-foot square concrete pier. The first level is painted black, the second and third levels are painted white, and the fourth level is black. The fifth-order Fresnel lens has a focal plane seventy-one feet above Lake Huron and is housed in a red roof lantern. The Poe Reef lighthouse marks the north side of the south channel of the Straits of Mackinac, while the Fourteen Foot Shoal Light marks the south side of the channel.

I am going to introduce to you one of those beacons, Round Island Lighthouse. In 1892, the Mackinac Point Lighthouse located in Mackinac City, now part of the state park, was built to ease vessel traffic from Lakes Huron, Michigan, and Superior. In 1894, the construction of Round Island Lighthouse was underway, located on the shoal off Round Island. The cost was $15,000, and it was completed in 1896. The three-story red brick building was home to the head keeper and two assistants. "First floor contained the boilers and compressors for the steam operated foghorn. Mounted on a shelf on the exterior of the second floor, Iron pipes piped up compressed air to the second floor. The second floor was where the keeper's kitchen, living room, dining room and one small bedroom. The third floor held three bedrooms and a service room, with access to the tower and lantern room by an iron ladder. It was equipped with a Fourth Order Fresnel lens; the lamp would show a steady white with a red flash every twenty seconds. The lamp was rotated with a clockwork occulting mechanism, which was powered by weights hanging in a weight pocket built into the wall" ("Round Island Lighthouse," *Seeing the Light*).

In 1924, the lighthouse became automated, no longer needing the services of the assistants. Their belongings were removed in 1939 when the Coast Guard assumed responsibility for the nation's lighthouses. From about 1924 to 1947, there was one keeper at Round Island. From 1934 to about 1938, there were two assistants on duty. In 1947, the automated Round Island Passage Light was built off the west harbor breakwater on

Mackinac Island. Round Island was no longer needed as a navigational aid and was abandoned. In 1958, Round Island became part of Hiawatha National Forest. The lighthouse now came under the care of the United States Forest Service. With the keepers and assistants gone, the inside began to deteriorate. On October 20, 1972, a violent storm blew so hard against the building that one lower corner of the building was broken away. "Many of the residents of Mackinac Island feared that the building would collapse and the poor impression that the deteriorating building left on the many visitors coming into the island harbor. A public desire to save the lighthouse began to surface" ("Round Island Lighthouse," *Seeing the Light*). For hundreds of years, these beacons of hope have saved countless lives. Now most are abandoned, and they need our help.

In 1974, the Round Island Lighthouse was placed on the National Register of Historical Places. For the past ten years, Boy Scout Troop 323 from Freeland, Michigan, has been working with the Lighthouse Keepers Association and the United States Forest Service, doing maintenance work on the lighthouse. The Boy Scouts spend a week each summer, working on the upkeep of the lighthouse. They are working to keep the lighthouse and associated outbuildings in working order. The United States Forest Service and the Boy Scouts have a working relationship: the USFS provides the project list, and the Boy Scout troop provides the manpower. It is not all work and no play; they get some time off. Some of the Boy Scouts spend their time on nearby Mackinac Island. The United States Forest Service (USFS) has been celebrating a centennial year; in recognition of this, the United States Congress recently granted money specifically to highlight the forests. Hiawatha applied for and received a $100,000 grant for work on the Round Island Lighthouse. A requirement for the grant was that Boy Scout Troop 323 matches all money. Now thanks to the Boy Scouts of Troop 323, Lighthouse Keepers Association, and the United States Forest Service, Round Island Lighthouse stands tall and proud, reminding us of the precarious waters that exist where ships have to pass on the Great Lakes. An interesting bit of information, Round Island Lighthouse was part of a scene in *Somewhere in Time*. The public can visit a majority of the 116 lighthouses. Some have museums open to the public, some are also private dwellings, and some serve as bed-and-breakfasts. Some of the lighthouses try to recruit volunteer keepers, who pay a fee to stay in the buildings for a week or more while guiding visitors through the sites.

Year Station Established   1896   Year Station Discontinued   1947

Also known as: ____   Rebuilt: _____   Auto :   1924

Position	Last Name	First Name	I	Born	Died	Start			End			Comment
						D	M	Year	D	M	Year	
Kpr.	Marshall	William				15	5	1896	11	2	1907	Rsgd.
1st Asst.	Schuster	Joseph				5	9	1896	1	11	1896	Trsfd.
1st Asst.	Carter	Arthur	M.			1	11	1896	1	4	1897	Trsfd. , Prmtd.
1st Asst.	Coarn	Albert				1	4	1897	14	8	1897	Rmvd.
1st Asst.	Gibbs	Jacob	H.		1913	30	3	1898	31	3	1907	Prmtd.
Kpr.	Gibbs	Jacob	H.		1913	1	4	1907	28	2	1911	Trsfd.
1st Asst.	Sweet	Garfield	L.			4	4	1907	13	7	1907	Trsfd.
1st Asst.	Coughlin	Peter				14	7	1907	12	5	1908	Trsfd. , Prmtd.
1st Asst.	Rice	John	H.			18	5	1908	3	6	1908	Rsgd.
1st Asst.	Breadlow	Theodore				3	7	1908	12	8	1909	Trsfd.
1st Asst.	Burzlaff	George	H.	1882	1958	18	8	1909	19	11	1912	Trsfd.
Kpr.	Smith	George	W.			1	3	1911			1914	Trsfd.
1st Asst.	Massicotte	Samuel					10	1912			1914	Dates unsure
Kpr.	Richardson	Clement	E.	1886				1914			1918	Trsfd. Dates unsure
Kpr.	Taylor	James	W.					1924	31	3	1927	Dates unsure
Kpr.	Henry	Charles				31	3	1927			1928	Dates unsure
1st Asst.	Bryant	Willis	C.	1898		6	12	1934			1937	End date unsure
1st Asst.	Proctor	Bert	T.	1893	1958			1937			1938	Prmtd. Dates unsure
Kpr.	Proctor	Bert	T.	1893	1958			1938			1947	Last Kpr.

Information compiled by Phyllis L. Tag of Great Lakes Lighthouse Research

This page last updated 11/17/2002.

DR. WILLIAM BEAUMONT

How many places are named after Dr. Beaumont?
About how many experiments did Dr. Beaumont
do on the digestive system?

Dr. William Beaumont's life was very interesting, in that he always wanted to be famous. He wanted to be posted in the frontier. It was as if he had a sense of destiny. There was no way that these two people, Dr. William Beaumont and Alexis St. Martin, would not otherwise meet up. They were about as different as two people can possibly be. Dr. William Beaumont liked the social life of high society; Alexis St. Martin was a voyageur and enjoyed his drinking. We will see how these two lives come together for medical history.

Dr. William Beaumont was born in Lebanon, Connecticut, on November 21, 1785. Parents Samuel and Lucretia had a total of nine children. His father was a farmer. Farmers very seldom become famous, and William wanted to be famous more than anything else. William tried his hand as a schoolteacher and did not like it. Later on, William's schoolmaster (and role model), Silas Fuller, who later on in life himself became a medical doctor in Lebanon, also served in the War of 1812 as regiment surgeon. He also tried clerking in a store and did not like it either. He decided on a career in medicine. Back then, there were too few colleges, let alone colleges of medicine. Instead they did what William did: they read under somebody; they read under the direction of an established doctor. He read about medical subjects. The doctor that he read under was Dr. Benjamin Moore of Champlain. He then had to pay for his apprenticeship with Dr. Benjamin Chandler and Dr. Truman Powell in Saint Albans, Vermont. In June 1812, the Third Medical Society of Vermont approved William to practice "physic and surgery." On September 13, 1812, at the young age of twenty-six, Dr. Beaumont entered the United States Army.

He enlisted as a surgeon's mate; it paid thirty dollars a month. He was assigned to the Sixth Infantry Regiment in Plattsburgh, New York. On April 13, Dr. Beaumont saw his first action of the War of 1812. The Sixth Regiment led the charge at York. Dr. Beaumont left the army after the war ended in June 1815 and started a private practice. Dr. Beaumont reentered the military in 1819. Dr. Beaumont was interested in staying in the army, provided he was given a frontier post, he told wartime friend Joseph Lowell, who later became surgeon general of the army. This time he was a surgeon and was stationed at Fort Mackinac.

Very little is known about Alexis St. Martin. His surname was Bidagan, and he was born in a small town in Quebec, Canada, about forty miles north of Montreal called Berthier, on April 18, 1794. His parents were Joseph Pierre Bidagan and Marie Des Agnes Angelique Guibeau. In 1822, Alexis was working as a voyageur for the American Fur Company. A voyageur was a traveling porter and canoe man, whose job it was to row the big cargo canoes along the rivers and to carry both the canoe and the cargo along the banks of the rivers when a waterfall or rapids got in the way. These men traveled in teams and faced their own special dangers. To this point, this is about all that is known about Alexis St. Martin.

On June 22, 1822, Alexis St. Martin, a French Canadian fur trader aged twenty-eight, was in the American Fur Company Store and was accidentally shot in the stomach. Dr. Beaumont was summoned. The patient was taken to the fort for further care. The wound did not heal completely, leaving a hole about the size of a quarter. Dr. Beaumont used this as an opportunity to conduct some experiments. Basically, what he did was that he took a silk string and tied different foodstuff to it and observed how the human stomach digested those different foodstuff. Four series of experiments were conducted at Forts Mackinac; Crawford; Washington, DC; and Plattsburgh—238 experiments in all. Dr. Beaumont was outlived by the patient by about seventeen years. Dr. Beaumont has three places named after him: Beaumont Army Medical Center, Fort Bliss, Texas; Beaumont, Texas; and Beaumont Medical Center, Royal Oak, Michigan.

What was learned from those experiments? Food digests most rapidly if it enters the stomach in small pieces. Gastric juices contain hydrochloric acid and pepsin; this was discovered in 1836 by Theodor Schwann. He opened the way to the new science of nutrition, the study of food and how the body makes use of it. One of the more interesting hobbies of Dr. Beaumont's was that he was extremely fond of music and dancing. Later in life when his hearing became impaired, he could not hear the music that his daughter was playing on the piano. When his daughter was playing the piano, he would sit with his teeth firmly fixed on the piano case. He would listen to his daughter play the piano through bone conduction. He could also keep in step on the dance floor as well.

In March 1853 while returning home from a visit to a patient late in the evening, he slipped and fell on the ice-covered stone steps. Striking his head with violence as he fell, with senses benumbed by the fall, he wandered about until met by a friend, who accompanied him to his home. He never recovered from the occipital hematoma, which became infected; his condition deteriorated, and he died on April 25, 1853. His good wife, Deborah, survived him by many years, and she died on January 23, 1870. Dr. Beaumont and his wife, Deborah, are buried in Bellefontaine Cemetery, Saint Louis, Missouri.

Alexis St. Martin lived fifty-eight years after the accident. Alexis St. Martin fathered seventeen children, and he did correspond with the Beaumont family time and again. When St. Martin died at the age of eighty-six on June 24, 1880, his family deliberately let the body decompose in the hot sun for four days and buried it deep in an unmarked grave in the churchyard, with rocks on top of the coffin. They wanted him to finally have peace. A committee finally persuaded one of St. Martin's granddaughters to disclose the location of the grave; a plaque was placed on the church's wall near the grave, stating that through his affliction, he served all humanity.

There was no way these two very different people would get together on their own accord. It was as if there was divine intervention. Dr. Beaumont was a man of destiny, knowing that he wanted to be famous. He was from the upper class. He was a doctor and in high standing and could be found at Magdelaine LaFramboise's residence at social parties. Alexis St. Martin was a voyager, and when he was not running the rivers, he could be found running and carousing around or could be found in the local tavern. The accident brought both of their lives together, forever tied together in history. They were tied by a shotgun blast in the American Fur Company Store. Theirs was a relationship, a bond between doctor and patient, just like any other, and they had their moments. There was no way that, if not for the stomach wound, these two people would have met. They were running in two different circles. Dr. Beaumont wanted to answer the questions, and Alexis wanted his family with him when traveling and also wanted to see family in France. This was where they would butt heads. In the end, they both shared a spot in medical history. And his family just wanted all the studying to end. They wanted him to rest in peace, and later he was recognized for his service to humanity.

THE FUR TRADE

Why was Michigan so important with regard to the fur trade?
Who was the country's first multimillionaire?
How many dollars' worth of fur went through the
American Fur Co. warehouse in 1822?

At some point in history, economic interests replaced religious conversions as a main goal of the French king and queen. Fur was the commodity of the era, just like oil is today. As you are about to see, there are tons of money involved, and it is a very ruthless game. We are going to look at how the fur trade evolved from two countries competing against one another, the fur trading companies and how they were warring against one another, how it got started on Mackinac Island, and how one giant in the fur trading business played a central role in Catholicism on the island.

For about two centuries, Michigan played a prominent role in the fur trade. Michigan became the desired location for two reasons. The geographical location and the abundance of the fur-bearing animals made her important. In the 1600s, the method of transportation was by using the waterways. Michigan was in the middle of the Great Lakes. Erie, Superior, Huron, and Michigan are the four great lakes that border Michigan. Michigan is cut in half by the Straits of Mackinac, which links the Lakes Huron and Michigan. The Straits is also connecting the east with the Mississippi River and its tributaries. Lake Superior would allow the fur traders access to the middle of the continent. Location was also important, because fearing the Iroquois, the French, when they were going to and from Montreal, would take the upper route; there was an upper route and a southern route. Fearing the Iroquois in the south, the French would avoid them by going up the Ottawa River, across by land to Lake Nispissing and down the French River to the Georgian Bay. From there they had access to Lake Huron and Lake Michigan, Wisconsin, Illinois, parts of the Mississippi, and eastern tributaries. Another important reason for Michigan being a desired location is the abundance of fur-bearing animals richly supplying trading posts in the important commerce.

At the start of the early 1600s, the priests from the Society of Jesus helped France establish a foothold in North America. They were called Jesuits. They were interested in bringing Christ to the First Nations. They explored, documented everything they saw and encountered, and mapped the frontier. The missionaries' beliefs in the importance of their cause carried them through the hardships. They helped the French settle and control the territory. The newly gained knowledge would prove useful later on for the fur trade. They had a hard time with some of the tribes when it came to trying to convert the Indians to Christianity. Some of the First Nations referred to the missionaries as Black Robes. A lot of times, the best intentions could not overcome the differences between Christianity and the beliefs of the Indians. Most of the First Nations were happy the way they were. They were not interested in change. In 1773, there were approximately 11 missionaries left in the Great Lakes region. The enemies of missionaries were soldiers, fur traders, and trappers. The missionaries were no longer welcome on the frontier. The fur trade quickly took over. The hardest thing the missionaries had to deal with was the soldiers and the fur traders persisting to give the Indians alcohol. They wanted the Indians to trade fur for it; the missionaries felt that it would destroy the Indian culture. A good drink could buy almost anything the Red Man had, for he was always thirsty. The Indian imbibed a taste and love for the white man's brandy, so strong that he would gladly exchange the costliest furs for a drink. Drunken brawls, lawlessness, and fraud were the natural outcomes, and while the missionary never ceased to rail against the evil, the trader taxed his brain to find some means of evading decrees or laws passed against it. The missionaries were the grunts of their day, breaking trails, mapping the entire region, building missions, doing all the exploring, and suffering hardship and loneliness. Alcohol was such a problem in 1633 the French government ordered that the sale of liquor was prohibited except under strong control. The other problem that they had to deal with was all the fur traders running around without licenses. The other problem was the soldiers who were trading contraband to the Indians as well. The French government could do little to enforce the decrees that they had against all this. They made decrees but could not enforce them.

In 1608, the city of Quebec was founded, which gave the French control of the Saint Lawrence River. It is important because it is a gateway to the interior of the North American Continent. In 1609, the Dutch took possession of the Hudson River Valley, another gateway to the interior. For the time being, both the French and the Dutch remained at their posts near the sea, exchanging furs for manufactured goods with the Indians. The French depended on the Huron and Algonquin. They lived north of the Saint Lawrence and the Great Lakes. The Dutch obtained their fur from the Iroquois. The Iroquois lived to the south of these waterways. Commercial competition between tribes led to war. The Iroquois went to war with the Algonquin and the Huron. The Iroquois eventually won, forcing the survivors to flee their lands. For a time, the French were trapped at their posts, and trapping came to a standstill. Peace was not restored until 1666. Reinforcements were brought in by the French; they defeated the Iroquois and took the fur trade west to the distant tribes out there.

This was around the time that economic interests took over religious interests. The king and queen of France were no longer interested in the conversion of natives to Christianity; they were interested in the monetary benefits of the fur trade. Governments struggled for influence in the region and juggled allies at all costs. In Europe, the fur-bearing animals had been basically trapped until they were extinct in most cases. The demand was still there. The beaver was in high demand because the fur will hold its shape, and hats are a long-lasting, sturdy means of protection from the ice and snow. A great deal of money was needed to finance trapping expeditions.

The French did not wish to underwrite the expense out of their national treasuries. What they did to encourage investors was that they were offered exclusive territorial rights to the North American fur trade. In return, the investor had to agree to establish a colony of settlers and pay a percentage of fur income to the government in taxes. In return, they had a monopoly on all the furs that were trapped in a certain area for a given period. Only the person holding the monopoly had a right to trade for furs in his designated area; that is how the grants worked. In the early days, they were awarded on a small scale. Later on they were expanded to newly formed companies with heavier financial backing.

Holders were given no help from the king other than their grant. They were left alone to operate pretty much as they wished. That made them very powerful and profitable. This was how the licensing process was handled. In Montreal or Quebec, the trader sells his beaver to a single buyer at a price fixed by the government, though trade in other pelts was less restricted. The means of transportation in those days was the birch-bark canoe and private trading vessels. These private trading vessels were small crafts; they could hold anywhere from two to fourteen men. When carrying merchandise, they were usually manned by three men and held a cargo of twenty hundred pounds.[1] Yet they were so light that a person could carry one on his back over the portages. The independent French trappers were called Coureurs de bois (rangers of the woods.) They were the unlicensed fur traders. They engaged in the fur trade without permission from the French authorities, mostly of French descent. Later on, a limited number of permits were issued to the Coureurs de bois, and they later became known as voyageurs. The voyageurs (traveler) were the licensed fur traders. They manned the canoes along well established routes and took the furs back to Montreal. They were also the ones who handled the transportation in the early days. When they had to portage around an obstacle, two men carried the canoe while the others carried the ninety-pound packs on their backs. There was such a huge demand for pelts that they never had to worry about a buyer.

Hivernants (Winterers) stayed in the back country over the winter and transported the trade goods from the rendezvous posts to farther away French outposts. The Hudson Bay Company was established in 1670. The French and their regulations helped the British get going in the fur trade. In 1660, two French fur traders, or coureurs, named Groseilliers and Radisson showed up in Montreal with a huge load of furs and descriptions of more land rich with furs in the northwest. The French officials reacted by confiscating the furs and fining them for hunting without a license. The two explorers, not at all happy with the turn of events, turned to King Charles II of Britain and offered him their knowledge of the area. They promptly received royal patronage. Hudson Bay Company became one of the most powerful fur companies of its time. The French had expanded their trading posts north of Lake Superior, into the Great Plains between Lake Michigan and the Rocky Mountains. They competed successfully with the British on the Hudson Bay.

From the beginning to the end of the fur trade, bitter warfare was waged for the possession of the "golden fleece" of the New World; monopolizing companies competed with coureurs de bois, Indian tribe with Indian tribe, French with English, English with Americans, independent traders with trading companies, and vice versa. It was a competition that lasted until there was almost no more to be had in the forest of the fur-bearing animals.

Fur trade was interrupted for about one year during Pontiac's uprising. With the columniation of hostilities, the fur trade began to pick up the pace, right where it left before hostilities. Problems were starting to show their ugly heads, problems such as liquor. Fur traders would land their canoes in the outskirts of the woods about three miles from the post, make bargains, and cheat the First Nations. All articles, even eggs, had to be

---

[1] *The Michigan Fur Trade*, p. 81. The author used the word *weight*.

purchased through them. They had the market cornered, and they made good use of it, charging exorbitant prices. The French still had a foothold on the region. Slowly but surely, the English was beginning to gain the advantage. The almighty dollar, like in the previous regime, was still the beaver pelt.

During the Revolution, there were at least three different things going on at once. First, we had the contest that was being waged among the individual fur traders. We had the American fur trader creeping in and trying to influence the fur trade. And we also had the unrest among the First Nations because of the Revolutionary War. When the war began, orders were issued that only the king's vessels carrying provisions should be allowed passage. This was a hard blow to the fur trade. They depended on provisions to trade with the First Nations; in return, the fur traders received pelts. Neither traders nor traders' supplies were allowed to go into the upper country without a pass from the military authorities. While the war for American independence was being waged, another conflict was waged within many frontier trading posts.

England's liberal policy of trade and success of her fur traders led to many unscrupulous adventurers. Men of many classes cared little for law and justice, so long as their undertaking prospered; these men had little respect for the rights of one another, much less for those of the First Nations. But they had to be considered as a rule; they alone furnished the coveted beaver pelt. One of the most effective means was to furnish them liquor. As early as 1762, there had been decrees to stop the flow of liquor to the First Nations. The merchants were clamoring for its repeal. Some of the members of the First Nations went as far as killing traders for refusing to sell liquor.[2] This was one way of getting pelts from the First Nations; another way was to undersell them and overbid rivals in trade. You had these merchants and traders who were acting on self-interest alone, exploiting traders and the First Nations for the largest immediate gain.

This rivalry brought with it a feeling of hostility so bitter that quarrels, fights, and murders became common. To many, it was not what means were used; where they could not drive them away, they could at least send them to a happier hunting ground. Here was genuine war being waged at all the frontier posts, all for a mere beaver pelt. They were willing to go after it by fair means or foul. This was going to be the ruination for all the independent fur traders.

The war caused great unrest among the First Nations; it also endangered the life of the fur traders. The rumor mill was at work at the frontier posts of men who had been killed by a warrior while on their way

---

[2] *Michigan Fur Trade*, p. 87. I found this one in the author's footnotes.

to the hunting grounds. Some of the murders were the natural outcome of a general unrest, and others were merited. There were those traders who considered the First Nations outside the realm of fair treatment, and they would be dealt with accordingly. The American Revolution was part of the influence. Some of the warriors favored and fought for the Americans. It also could be like during the French and Indian War; they fought alongside the French, so now they would fight alongside the British. For whatever reasons, these murders had the attention of the fur traders. The English and the French alike informed the First Nations that until they straightened up and ceased their depredations, no traders were going out to them. The white man had many things they coveted and had cultivated a taste for. It was going to be a while for the First Nations to settle down. The war ended and threw their world into even more turmoil. The British traders in Michigan were not idle, and it behooved the British to gather as much fur or pelts as they could and as fast as they could, for the days the British had sovereignty over this part of the frontier were numbered. It was starting to become very evident that for each trader to pursue their own interest, with no regard or concern for others, was disastrous for all.

Now we are starting where the British and American governments are trying to get a handle on this fur trade free for all. In 1779, Ezekiel Solomon and others petitioned Major DePeyster, their commandant, permission to establish a general store in which all traders might place their goods and pool the receipts. Permission was granted.

There were some rules for those who wanted to be a part of it. All the traders belonging would put their merchandise together for trading purposes, each securing a share of the proceeds in proportion to their stock. All the members belonging promised, under penalty of losing their goods, to abandon private trade with the First Nations or with any other person who might hurt the company. Those who were qualified for dealing with the First Nations were to be chosen by general vote of the members. If the choice was approved by the commandant, these members were obliged to go where he permitted the members of the company to send them. This would ultimately end in failure, because the term of the agreement would dissolve or expire in 1780. For now, the free-for-all continues. There was another attempt at union among the fur traders, but it also ended in failure.

There were two companies that would come to form and become a prominent influence in the fur trade. They were the North West and the Mackinaw Companies. They were just for trading purposes. The North West Company was founded in 1783. It was fully organized and operational in 1787. When this organization first launched into the field of the fur trade, the association was more or less in the nature of an experiment. The North West Company was not without its stations of trade in Michigan, but its main depot for the western commerce was located at Grand Portage. Naturally, it drew its suppliers from the west and northwest. The Mackinaw Company was founded by 1783–84. It was supposed to have been comprised of some of the same mercantile firms as composed the North West Company. It operated largely through the American Territory, having principal station at Mackinaw, where it drew its name. Michigan was where the Mackinaw Company got its share of commerce, but also a good portion of it came from the regions of Lake Superior and Mississippi. A war had been waged between trader and trader, a war that was bitter and unceasing, because the opponents were equally matched. The formation of companies did not put an end to this war; the contestants only changed. This was where there was struggle between individual traders and a powerful business. This individual trader usually was swept off the field of play or forced to combine interests with a large business. They could also continue their operations as an independent, and many were able to hold their own against the big operations. Here, too, competition had to be encountered, for the fur trade was still an all-important occupation of the day in this section of the Western world.

The harvest of furs, reaped by the British traders in Michigan during this regime, was a small task. The treaty of peace had been signed by the British, both the Treaty of Paris and the Jay Treaty. Traders still roamed about the Michigan forests, bartering for Michigan furs, cheating the First Nations of Michigan. This fur trade was an important plum, and a sweet one at that, too juicy to drop to the victorious Americans. This was why the British held on to its possessions until after the signing of the Jay's Treaty in 1795. In October 1796, the United States took possession of Fort Mackinac. Fur trade was still in the hands of the British. The two fur trading firms, the North West and the Mackinaw Companies, most of their members were British subjects. The Mackinaw Fur Trading Company had a death grip in Michigan and the Lake Superior fur trade. The War of 1812 put a halt to the fur trade, until the end of the hostilities in 1815.

At this point, we have two systems of fur trade; we have the factory fur trading company and then there is the independent, all at work, competing for the same prize. The factory system was an attempt by the United States to control the trade to the First Nations. The factory system was put in place by the Americans for two reasons: to keep the First Nations supplied with goods and for protection and justice against the extreme greed of the traders. No alcohol was allowed in these factories. The price for the goods was governed; no bad merchandise was to be sold to the First Nations. All goods in the trading house were meant for the First Nations at cost, and if purchased by others, they were to pay at an advance of 10 percent. These factories were built to establish a relationship with the First Nations. These trading houses were running for two years and then revived again in 1802 and then finally abolished in 1822.

The French were the first Europeans to the Great Lakes Region, by the missionaries and then the fur traders and soldiers. For a period of time, we also had the French and the British competing for the pelts, then we had the British, then the British and the Americans, and in the end, it was the Americans. It was a cutthroat business, no-holds-barred, bloody war, man against man, man against the business—it was war. At one point, we had the French and Indian war before the French and Indian war was even started. The French and the British were having confrontations over the fur trade before 1763, which was the beginning of the Seven Years' War, also known as the French and Indian War. The French, because of their tendency for close intermingling with the First Nations and often intermarrying with their women, got along real well the First nations, except for the Iroquois Nation, comprising of five nations. The five Iroquois nations, characterizing themselves as "the people of the longhouse," were the Mohawk, Oneida, Onondaga, Cayuga, and Seneca. After the Tuscarora joined in 1722, the confederacy became known to the

English as the Six Nations and was recognized as such at Albany, New York (1722).

They had become dependent on the trade goods brought by the French. The early British traders moved about among the First Nations for years, establishing their honesty and gaining their trust. The later arrivals seemed to go out of their way to cheat the trading members of the First Nations in any way possible, like the poor quality of goods they sold; they wore out and fell apart quickly. Food goods were tainted or diluted. When it came to liquor, the Indians could hardly resist. It fired them into an uncontrollable act, which was soon gone, with nothing to show for it except a headache. The problem was that the First Nations had complaints to the authorities, which had no effect, so they were really left with no other option; they began attacking the new traders. The allegiance of the First Nations was swinging back to the French because of the cheating and everything else that was going on between the First Nations and the British. At this point, John Jacob Astor came into the picture with his entrepreneurial skills and importing and exporting know-how.

JOHN JACOB ASTOR

John Jacob Astor was born in Waldorf, Germany, in 1763. He was the youngest son of a butcher. He was an assistant in his father's business, as a dairy salesman. In 1784, he landed in Baltimore, Maryland. He made his way to New York, where his other brother, Henry, lived, where he had established a butcher shop. In 1786, he opened up his own shop and often traveled to the wilderness to procure furs for his business, trading fur to the Native Americans in his fur goods shop. On September 19, 1785, Astor married Sarah Cox Todd. She possessed a frugal mind and a business judgment that he declared better than that of most merchants. She assisted him in the practical details of his business.

The signing of the Jay Treaty between England and the United States in 1794 opened up the markets in Canada and the Great Lakes Region. Astor at once made contact with the North West Company based in Montreal, who was a rival with Hudson Bay Company based out of London. Astor imported furs from Montreal to New York and then shipped them to Europe. He also imported and exported to China. In 1807, the US Embargo Act disrupted Astor's import/export business. With permission from President Thomas Jefferson, John Jacob Astor established the American Fur Company on April 6, 1808. Later on he would establish the Pacific Fur Company and the Southwest Fur Company. The Columbia River Trading Post, at Fort Astoria, was the first US community on the Pacific Coast.

With the start of the War of 1812, the men at Fort Astoria panicked, selling the business and its holdings to a Canadian-based company, the North West Company. It turned out their fears were well founded. Just months later, a British warship arrived with the intention of occupying the fort. Astor's northwest dreams were dashed; the Astors sold their fort to the Canadian North West Company in 1813, and the British would maintain control of the outpost for the next forty years. When Congress passed an 1816 bill barring non-US citizens from owning fur businesses in

US territory, the same Canadian company that had purchased Fort Astoria was forced to sell all their holdings below the Great Lakes to Astor. He helped persuade Congress in 1816 to pass an act excluding Canadians from the American fur trade unless employed by an American company. Astor then bought out the holdings of the North West Company inside American territory for a fraction of its worth. The company was, at that point engaged, in a struggle with the Hudson Bay Company and was in no condition to defend itself. Six years later, Astor received additional aid from the US government when Congress voted to close all trading posts operated by foreign governments, leaving Astor with a near monopoly on the fur trade.

William Backhouse Astor was born on September 19, 1792, in New York, New York. While his lobbying of Congress continued, Astor briefly turned his attention away from the fur trade. In 1816, he purchased ten tons of opium from the Ottoman Empire (modern-day Turkey) and shipped it to Canton, China, aboard one of his American Fur Company ships—despite China's banning of the drug seventeen years earlier. After turning a tidy profit on the illegal enterprise, Astor abruptly ended his involvement in 1819. Astor was the first American known to traffic the drug in China, but certainly not the last. Several early American fortunes were built on the Chinese opium trade.

Though he had dabbled in real estate speculation on earlier occasions, Astor's first big land deal came in 1807, when former Vice President Aaron Burr was arrested for treason for his involvement in a plot to annex territory in Louisiana and Mexico to establish an independent republic. The financially beleaguered Burr, who had already heavily mortgaged his Manhattan estate, known as Richmond Hill, appealed to Astor for help. Burr had been acquitted, but his reputation was in ruins, and he sought a new start in Europe. Desperate for cash, he agreed to transfer the deed to Richmond Hill to Astor for just $32,000—in what Burr later maintained was to be a temporary agreement. Astor, of course, saw nothing temporary about the transaction. The second son of John Jacob Astor, John Jacob II, struggled with mental illness and was in no position to take a leading role in his father's work. Soon after his arrival in New York, William became a partner in the firm Jacob Astor & Son. Though he was a partner, he mostly followed his father's instructions in the running of the business. Even when he served as head of the American Fur Company, it reportedly was his father who decided when and how to sell the company's holdings.

When John Jacob Astor died in March 1848, his will contained bequests for several charitable groups plus approximately $400,000 ($10 million in today's dollars) for the creation of a free public library to be built in what is now New York's East Village neighborhood. The Astor Library became one of the most well-respected institutions in the city, but the lack of additional financial support from the Astor family left it struggling financially. In 1895, the Astor collection merged with that of another New York philanthropist, James Lenox, and utilizing the funding left by yet another former New York governor Samuel Tilden, created the New York Public Library system. The main-branch library, on Forty-Second Street and Fifth Avenue, opened in 1911, and for more than a century, the entrance has been guarded by two marble lions—originally known as Leo Astor and Leo Lenox after the library's benefactors but now are more popularly known as Patience and Fortitude.

Upon his father's death, William Astor became the richest man in the United States, inheriting roughly $18 million in 1848. Like his father, William invested in New York City real estate. Due to his vast holdings, he earned the nickname Landlord of New York. He also took care of his brother, John Jacob Astor II. The American Fur Company came to dominate trading in the area around the Great Lakes in 1822. In June 1822, $3,000,000 worth of fur went through the American Fur Company. Astor retired from the American Fur Company and withdrew from both domestic and foreign trade in 1834. After 1800, he concentrated on real estate in New York City. He profited not only from the sale of lands and rents but also from the increasing value of lands within the city. During the last decade of his life, his income from rents alone exceeded $1,250,000. His total wealth was estimated at $20–30 million (the greatest source being his land holdings on Manhattan Island) at his death. Astor, the wealthiest man in country at that time, died on March 29, 1848. At his death, his fortune was estimated to be about $20 million, the bulk of which went to his son William Backhouse Astor. Astor left the bulk of his fortune to his second son William, because his eldest son, John Jr., was sickly and mentally unstable. Astor left enough money to care for John Jr. for the rest of his life. Driven to succeed, John Jacob Astor built a family and a fortune that became a part of American history. Aside from such charitable donations as the library, John Jacob Astor left the bulk of his $20 million fortune (estimated by *Forbes* magazine to be worth more than $100 billion today) to his second son, William Backhouse Astor Sr. To ensure the continuation of his family's wealth, however, Astor planned ahead. In 1834, he created what's believed to be America's first family trust, consisting of 125 parcels of valuable real estate covering much of the west side of midtown Manhattan. The Astors' control of such a large portion of Manhattan real estate led to the coining of one of the family's nicknames—the Landlords of New York.

SOME FACTS

In 1893, William Waldorf Astor opened up the thirteen-story Waldorf Hotel, at the corner of Fifth Avenue and Thirty-Third.

In 1897, the Waldorf was joined by the seventeen-story Astoria Hotel by John Jacob Astor IV.

In 1912, John Jacob Astor IV died tragically on the *Titanic* on April 15, 1912.

In 1929, a decision was made to sell the site to the developers of what would become the Empire State Building and to tear down the hotel in 1929.

In 1931, the second Waldorf-Astoria Hotel opened in its current location on Park Avenue on October 1, 1931, as the tallest and largest hotel in the world.

COURTHOUSE

"A man's home is his castle" was used as an argument
in what court case on Mackinac Island?
Who was accused of murder in the case?
How is the courthouse used today?
Before Pond's case, how many notable cases
were there at the court house?

The present city hall of the city of Mackinac Island, Michigan,
is the original building constructed in 1839 as the Mackinac County
Courthouse. It succeeded the County Territorial Courthouse built many
years before, according to local historians. The 1839 building followed
the administration of the state into the Union by two years. Constructed
in 1839, the Michilimackinac County Courthouse on Mackinac Island,
Michigan, continues to serve as the island's police station, town hall, and
town court. In 1882, the county seat was transferred from Mackinac Island,
where it had been since the beginning of US government administration,
during the height of the fur trade boom. At that time, Michigan Territory
was still a barely settled frontier wilderness, and Mackinac Island, then
called Michilimackinac, was given jurisdiction over all the eastern Upper
Peninsula, all the northern Lower Peninsula, and all the islands in Lake
Michigan and Lake Huron that were assigned to the United States by
the Treaty of Paris that ended the Revolutionary War. The first county
courthouse must have been successful, because in 1823, Congress ordered
that the local circuit court start holding annual sessions there. One of the
goals of the new state government of 1837 was to whip all its counties into
line and make them provide themselves with an infrastructure that would
live up to the standards of the East Coast. When Michilimackinac County
built its new courthouse in 1839, they selected a federal-style design with
a proud little cupola and flagpole.

There are a couple of notable court cases on Mackinac Island. One of the cases involved some seven Native Americans. They were thrown in jail for murder and housed in the jail on the island. Later on, they escaped by a canoe that was abandoned and made their way to Green Bay. The first Mackinac County courthouse was also the site of the first jury trial of Private James Brown, the Fort Mackinac soldier who was tried and convicted for the 1828 murder at the fort of his commanding officer. That trial would be tried in Green Bay; the execution would be carried out on Mackinac Island

Pond's Defense

Augustus Pond, a fisherman from nearby Seul Choix, was convicted of manslaughter in this building in 1859. In 1860, the Michigan Supreme Court reversed Pond's conviction, clarifying a legal principle of self-defense that is followed to this day.

Isaac Blanchard and two confederates had, for three days, challenged Pond, his family, and Pond's hired hands, Cull and Whitney. One night, the three began tearing down Pond's net house and attacked Cull, who was sleeping inside. Pond confronted the men and, upon hearing Cull's cries, called out, "Leave, or I'll shoot." The three men continued, and Pond fired, killing Blanchard. A jury sitting here sentenced Pond to ten years' confinement at hard labor.

Michigan Supreme Court Justice James V. Campbell, a towering figure in the state's legal history, wrote the historic decision overturning the conviction. Justice Campbell stressed that a man's home is his castle: "Human life is not to be lightly disregarded, and the law will not permit it to be destroyed unless upon urgent occasion." This, Justice Campbell wrote, was such an occasion. "A man is not, however, obliged to retreat if assaulted in his dwelling, but may use such means as are absolutely necessary to repel the Assailant and to prevent his forcible entry, even to the taking of life . . . [unless] he can otherwise arrest or repel the assailant." The issue remains difficult, but Justice Campbell's reasoning continues, as it has for generations, to guide our courts and juries. The plaque was placed by the State Bar of Michigan and the Fiftieth Judicial Circuit Bar Association (1995).

The principle of self-defense set down by the Supreme Court's decision in *People v. Pond* has been reaffirmed several times since in Michigan law. As recently as 2006, the Michigan legislature passed a Self-Defense Act that put into statute many of the elements set forth by this decision, now almost 150 years old, in justifying the use of deadly force in extreme circumstances to defend one's home or property in Michigan.

The Forts

What was the importance of all three forts?
Name the three different nations that have flown flags at the forts?
What were some of the different roles the forts have played in history?
When was Michigan's first treaty with the First
Nations? And how much did that land cost?

Fort De Baude (Fort Saint Ignace). In the autumn of 1672, a great war party of northern tribes under the general leadership of the Ottawas of Manitoulin was on the warpath against the Sioux to the Southwest. With them were the Hurons, the Pottawatomies, the Sacs, and the Foxes. They suffered a disastrous defeat in what is now northern Wisconsin. In what is now the Saint Croix Valley, where the battle took place, the attacking expedition met an enemy who drove them to a rout and retreat. The invaders fled back north in a winter marked by severe weather and unspeakable suffering. Those who died became cannibal food supply for the survivors. None of the party would have returned alive had it not been for the rear guard action of the Huron, covering the retreat of the war party. The survivors made it back to Saint Ignace, established a village, and constructed a log fort. It was constructed in the vicinity where Father Marquette and Father Dablon had established a mission two years prior. Commanders of the fort and district were selected by the governor general of New France. At this time between 1678 and 1681, it was becoming apparent to the French government at Montreal that great possibilities of profit existed in the increasing fur trade with the Indians of the northwest, centering in the struggling settlement at Saint Ignace, and a military detail of French soldiers was sent to occupy Fort Saint Ignace (Fort De Baude) under the command of M. de Villeraye, first-listed French officer in the available records.

He was in charge not only of the meager fortifications but also of the supervision of the fur trade and Coureurs de bois that traded upon lakes and southern countries of Canada. He was commandant until 1684, when he was relieved. This next commandant realized the situation with the relationship between the First Nations and the French. His name was Commandant La Durantaye.

The Iroquois were on the warpath in other parts of the French territory, with an eye on the Straits area. The Iroquois were in close alliance with the British, both commercial and military. They were looking northwest with covetous eyes on the increasing value and importance of the French fur trade. In 1684, Sieur Daniel Greysolon, the king of the Coureurs de bois, joined Nicolas Perrot in enlisting with La Durantaye in an expedition against the distant Iroquois, leaving an officer by the name of Valtrie in command back in Saint Ignace. The French forces scored a decisive victory over the Iroquois.

La Durantaye returned to the region, hoping that the confidence of his First Nation neighbors would be restored as to the potent power of the French king. There is little doubt that had the expedition failed, the wavering northern tribes would have deserted to the English. Commandant Durantaye and his linguist Nicolas Perrot addressed themselves to the task, regaining the friendship of the First Nations, who had been weaned away by English advances.

Of all the post in the territory at that time, Fort Saint Ignace was probably the most important, because everything coming to or from Wisconsin and beyond had to pass by this post. There was an enemy lurking among the fort though. The enemy was not a threat from the outside; the threat was from the inside, in the form of trafficking of brandy, or "fire water," between the French garrison as well as the traders and the First Nations. The trading of brandy to the First Nations was a point of major contention between the missionaries, the fur traders, the garrison at the fort, and the government in Montreal and the King of France. They could not agree to disagree if they tried. King Louis XIV forbade the transportation of brandy into Michigan. Missionaries were definitely against the transportation of the brandy into Michigan as well. Royal decrees and threats from afar meant very little to those in the frontier of North America. So the governor and commandants winked at its importation and sale, and the blame was heaped on the shoulders of the coureurs de bois.

The law that prohibited liquor was falling pretty much on deaf ears. There was also another law that was falling on deaf ears, the law that only licensed traders could trade fur; accordingly, illicit commerce prevailed everywhere. A soldier's life at the fort, his occupation, as well as that of the commandant were the trade with the First Nations, a trade that legally belonged to the regularly licensed voyageurs.

With this, you can imagine that there was practically no discipline among the soldiers. The best way for me to put what was going on is like this: The French army at Fort Saint Ignace, at this point, sort of resembled the American army before Valley Forge. That winter at Valley Forge, General Friedrich von Steuben arrived and brought discipline and esprit de corps to the American army. This practice of fur traders ran amok and could only have one outcome. That outcome was that there was a glut in the beaver pelt market, and prices fell. There was no end in sight to the goings-on at the fort. At the close of the seventeenth century, Michigan's forests were filled with illicit fur traders. At the beginning of the eighteenth century, a strong rival was emerging in the Lower Peninsula to dispute the monopoly of the Michigan fur trade and the abandonment of Fort Saint Ignace.

The fort was abandoned for a time and moved down to Fort Detroit. The commandant was Antoine de la Cadillac. Cadillac encouraged the Odawas and the Hurons to leave the Straits area and go down and build homes in the vicinity of Detroit. Several thousand followed Cadillac to Detroit. In despair, the Jesuits burned the Saint Ignace mission buildings and returned to Montreal in 1705. The fort remained relevant and actually permitted the inhabitants to trade on condition that they pay a small tax. The abandonment of the strategically located Fort Saint Ignace was a source of great embarrassment for the governor general of Canada.

Sometime between 1706 and 1708, he persuaded Father Marest to return to Saint Ignace. Following the Father would be former commandant Louvigny and a company of men as well. This commandant was endorsed, much respected and loved by the First Nations. He was also an intelligent and vigilant officer. Even back then, the red tape was horrendous, because Father arrived in 1708, and the promised military contingent did not arrive until 1712. A little bit after his arrival to the Straits area, he found a new location at Mackinaw City, the northern point of what is now the Lower Peninsula of Michigan.

The French now had a fort, garrison, trading post, and a mission. Even though more of the wilderness was available for trade, at the same time, competitive posts had come to be. A more powerful force was at work in hindering the commerce in the wilderness; it was war, both intertribal and intercolonial. There was a lot of trouble at all the posts in the late '40s, but there seemed to be more trouble in this section of the territory for some reason. War not only endangered the life of the trader but also lessened and made his trade unprofitable. In 1759, the British army defeated the French in the Battle of Quebec. It tolled the last bell for the French control of Canada and the Northwest. The British came at once, and within a year, a garrison marched through the gates of Michilimackinac. Commandant Captain Monsieur de Beaujeu evacuated the post in October 1760. He retired to Illinois, with four officers, two cadets, forty-eight soldiers, and seventy-eight militia men.

Fort Michilimackinac (Mainland). In October 1760, British soldiers arrived to take over the fort. These soldiers were under the Command of Major George Etherington. He served with distinction with General Wolfe on the Plains of Abraham and in the capture of Quebec. The soldiers that he arrived with were split up into different details to occupy the remaining posts that the French surrendered. He summoned the inhabitants of the surrounding area, and he asked them to sign their allegiance to the Crown. In 1763, King George III declared that all trade with the First Nations should be free and open to every one of his subjects, provided they have a license from the governor or commander in chief of the colony in which they lived and obeyed and observed all trade regulations.

The British had a freer trade policy. This policy later on would lead to scheming and underselling in trade, a competition that brought on lawlessness and bitter feuds, until the wiser traders, from sheer desperation, sought to combine their interests to protect trade. Thus came into play the great fur trading companies. After the war with the British in what is known as the French and Indian War in 1760, the French lost, so they had to give up all their territory east of the Mississippi.

At this time, we had the French and the British, the world's two superpowers, involved in the fur trade on the North American continent. When the French were running things, they had somewhat of a congenial relationship with the First Nations. They would trade with them, eat with them, and often marry into the tribes. With the British, it was more of an adversarial relationship; they often would cheat them and treat them as third-class citizens. Pontiac was one of two chiefs in American history who was to get the First Nations to stop fighting among themselves and make a concerted effort to defeat the expansion of the white man westward. The other one was Crazy Horse. He would come later on in history, defeating General George Armstrong Custer at the Little Bighorn River.

We will not be concerning ourselves with Crazy Horse at all. A lot of the First Nations had sided with the British during the French and Indian War and, in consequence, lost a lot of tribal members. They had fear or concern of the uncontrolled English settlement and expansion of their lands, or land encroachment. They were also looking for some redress, or compensation for the sacrifices made. The French had compensated the First Nations, but King George was not going to compensate them. Well, with that decision, the British were about to pay in blood and in goods looted from the forts.

In the uprising, Pontiac laid siege to, or took over and burned and looted, not just the three forts in Michigan, but elsewhere in the Great Lakes region as well. Fort Saint Joseph, on May 25, 1763, was attacked and destroyed. The commander and three soldiers were taken prisoner, and later they were exchanged at Detroit in July. The British would not garrison the fort after the uprising. There were warning signs and rumors of trouble milling about the territory. Some commanders listened and paid attention, while others did not. That was the difference in the outcomes of the two forts here in Michigan. In Fort Detroit, on May 1, Pontiac and forty to fifty warriors went to Detroit under the pretense of meeting with Major Gladwin. Most were performing a ceremonial dance. The rest were scouting the fort for defenses and location of supplies. When the ceremony was over, Pontiac said he would return in a few days.

On May 7, Pontiac and sixty trusted warriors would enter the fort and ask to meet with Major Gladwin. They would carry weapons hidden underneath blankets, spreading themselves out around the inside of the fort, and at a given signal, they would attack, being careful not to harm any of the French. On May 6, Major Gladwin got word of Pontiac's treachery that was about to be played out in his fort. It is not known who warned Gladwin of what was about to happen. Two possibilities were Catherine, a Native American who was making a pair of moccasins for Major Gladwin, and the other was a French resident who saw the Native Americans shortening the barrels of their guns and warned Major Gladwin what he saw.

On the morning of the seventh, all the French inhabitants of the fort were not to be found anywhere. At around ten in the morning, Pontiac, along with three hundred blanket-clad Indians, entered the fort under the watchful eyes of the soldiers standing ready around the inside the fort with fixed bayonets. Seeing the preparations, the signal was never given. Pontiac was bound and determined to take the largest post of the Upper Great Lakes. Pontiac laid siege to the fort. Lucky for the British, they were able to resupply the fort using the Detroit River. Try as they might, the First Nations could not come up with a solution to that problem of resupplying Fort Detroit, and Fort Detroit was a bust for the First Nations. The siege would continue until October 31, 1763.

On December 10, 1762, the Fort Repentigny, Sault Sainte Marie, fire destroyed the fort. Lt. John Jamet and his detachment of ten men marched through fifty miles of ice and snow and made it safely. Where the garrison was transferred to Fort Michilimackinac, transfer was completed in February 1763. News of the uprising had not made its way north yet, nearly four hundred miles by canoe from Detroit. The local Chippewa tribe knew of it through Pontiac. They eventually staged one of the most cleverly devised strategies to capture the British forts. Michilimackinac was the major fur trading center on the Upper Great Lakes; therefore, it had a larger garrison. There were three officers and anywhere from thirty-five to thirty-seven men. With Lieutenant Jamet's detachment, we have four officers and forty-five to forty-seven men. The commandant was Capt. George Etherington. Laurent Du Charme, Lt. Charles Langlade, and Alexander Henry, all had informed Captain Etherington of the unrest of the First Nations. Capt. Etherington disregarded the information and threatened "to send the next person who should bring a story of the same kind a prisoner to Detroit." On the morning of July 2, 1763, from four hundred to six hundred tribal members of the Chippewa Nation gathered at the fort for a game of *baggataway* (lacrosse) against some visiting Sauks. Despite all the warnings, Capt. Etherington did not place the fort on alert. While soldiers watched the game outside the open gates, women from the tribes meandered next to the stockade. Unbeknown to the soldiers, underneath the woolen blankets, the kind for the time of year, they hid the weapons. As the game progressed, the players "accidently" threw the ball near the gate of the fort. Players rushed inside, seemingly to retrieve it. As they were running into the fort after the ball, the weapons were being handed out. Captain Etherington, a couple of other officers, and eleven or twelve soldiers were quickly captured and were quickly whisked away. A handful of fur traders, including Alexander Henry, were also taken prisoner.

The Odawas were incensed at the Chippewas for not including them in the plan to capture the fort. The Odawas had received the war belt from Pontiac, encouraging them to join the uprising, but had not yet come to a decision on June 2, when the Chippewas struck the fort. On June 4, the Odawas arrived at the fort, immediately taking all the prisoners from the Chippewas. After a two-day conference, the Odawas were given some plunder from the fort. Four soldiers and one trader were bartered for the plunder. Capt. Etherington and another officer, eleven soldiers, and two traders went to Cross Village to another village southwest of the fort along Lake Michigan. Later Etherington and the combined contingent were escorted to Montreal by the Odawas on August 13, after thirty-two days. For a while, the fort was occupied by French traders. Sir William Johnson, superintendent of British Northern Indian Department, negotiated a peace treaty in a council at Niagara. It was followed by the reoccupation of Fort Michilimackinac in August 1764. On July 23, 1767, Pontiac signed a peace treaty. In 1769, a Peoria warrior killed Pontiac by striking him in the back of the head with a hatchet. The challenge was not only negotiating a peace, but enforcing it was another challenge in itself. Tensions would continue and, in some ways, contributed to severing of the umbilical cord from England by the colonists about ten years later.

When you talk about Pontiac's Uprising, there is a character that has to be talked about. It is Alexander Henry. In 1762, Alexander Henry set off on his adventure from Montreal, Canada, in a canoe to Cross Village. Later on in the fall, he canoed up to Sault Sainte Marie, where he had plans on staying the winter. In December, the fort caught fire and was completely destroyed. The fire saved them from the same fate as Fort Saint Joseph and Michilimackinac. The garrison, along with Alexander Henry, returned to Fort Michilimackinac. They arrived on December 31, 1762; the next day, navigation was closed on the Straits. During the spring, the First Nations were growing restless and showing hostilities toward the British. On June 2, a group of warriors gathered outside the fort for a game of *baggataway*. Unbeknown to the British soldiers, underneath the cloaks that the squaws were wearing, they were concealing weapons. The ball was "accidently" thrown toward the open gate. While they were rushing after the ball, the weapons were being handed out. A dozen or two officers, soldiers, and traders, including Alexander Henry, were taken prisoner. While at Fort Michilimackinac, Alexander Henry was friends and became blood brothers with a chief by the name of Wawatum. Wawatum bought Alexander Henry's freedom with lots of gifts.

The warriors, after the attack and after the celebration, realized the British would want to exact some sort of revenge for the attack on their fort and the slaughter of soldiers and traders. They went to Mackinac Island, where they could defend themselves better. Wawatum took Alexander Henry and headed to the interior of the island. While walking to the destination, warriors intercepted two traders who had rum and commenced consuming the rum. Wawatum took his friend to the only place he would be safe from the drunken warriors, admitting that he himself could not resist. After walking about a half of a mile, they came to a rock face with a small opening. "This is where you will make your lodge until I return" was the instructions by Wawatum to Alexander Henry. He broke branches and boughs and used them to sleep on, wrapping himself in his blanket.

The next morning, he woke up with a crick in his back. Wondering why and looking around, he came quickly to the conclusion that the cave in which he was staying in was used for some sort of burial ground.

Whole-body skeletons were everywhere, just body parts. It was as if the whole body was thrown in the cave. The rest of the time, he decided to lodge underneath a bush. This went on for about three nights and three days. For about a year, Alexander Henry and Wawatum traveled throughout the area, gradually making their way through Canada, to Fort Niagara. Alexander Henry returned to the region with the British expeditionary force. They were relieving and reoccupying posts along the frontier. As you can see, he made it through the ordeal unscathed. He did get fed up with the Great Lakes region, where he moved to and settled down in Montreal, Canada. He lived to the age of eighty, which was unheard of back then, and went on to author a book titled *Attack at Michilimackinac 1763*.

In August 1764, Capt. William Howard arrived at Fort Michilimackinac. Two years later, on August 10, 1766, Maj. Robert Rogers arrived, along with his wife, Elizabeth, and became commandant of Fort Michilimackinac. One of Rogers's ambitions while at Michilimackinac was searching for the Northwest Passage. Even though he never would get official approval, he did send a party out, and they made it 250 miles west of Lake Winnipeg. That was as far as it would get due to lack of supplies. Rogers never gave up on trying to get the support and funding until the outbreak of the American Revolution, which brought his dream to a final end. If he had gained the support and funding necessary, he could very well have been the first to cross the continent, fifty years before Lewis and Clark.

While his expedition was underway for the Northwest Passage, on August 18, he met with local Odawa chiefs for continued peace. In return, they were promised more open trade policies and presented them with a traditional beaded wampum belt. They retired to consider the terms and conditions and returned and accepted them. A beaded belt was given to Rogers the following day, along with promises of peace and friendship. On September 20, Rogers met with the more hostile Chippewa, essentially giving them the same message. They replied that they had never been able to trust Captain Howard. Now that Rogers was in command, they hoped that things would improve. As a symbol of goodwill, they turned a war belt over to him that the Shawnee and Delaware had sent, calling a resumption of hostilities that very summer. The following summer, on July 2, 1767, representatives from the Menominee, Winnebago, Sauk, Fox, Odawa, Mississauga, Chippewa, and the Sioux all met at Fort Michilimackinac. All professed their friendship for the English, and more important was the peace between the Chippewa and the Sioux. They had been at war with one another for over forty years. Ending the war among them would go a long way in helping out the English trade and would also help put a stop to the growing Spanish and French influence in the region. The negotiating of this treaty was Rogers's greatest successes while at Michilimackinac. When Rogers was dealing with the First Nations, he had shown himself to be firm, but fair, and recognized their basic character and needs. Rogers was commandant of probably the most important post of the frontier. He was responsible for the trade with the First Nations and also the relations. He governed over the British and the French civilians, and he did it with great success. The success came at a price, however; it placed him in conflict with Gage and Johnson. Both saw him as a threat to their own interests. General Gage replaced Major General Amherst, commandant of His Majesty's troops in North America, with Sir William Johnson as superintendent of British Northern Indian Department. Both men had large financial stakes in the development of the land recently acquired from France and the large flow of commerce that would follow. Before Rogers even took command of Michilimackinac, Gage had knowledge of some letters asking Rogers to defect and join the French, and he would be justly compensated. This was one of several letters that was sent to Rogers. One of these letters was intercepted; it was read by both Gage and Johnson then resealed and sent on to Rogers. Rogers in turn notified Gage of the letter. The letter was sent to Gage, but the canoe carrying the letter sank. At this point, Gage and Johnson were just looking for an excuse to have him relieved of command. They finally made their move on December 6, 1767. He was placed under arrest in irons and confined to the fort's guardhouse. He spent the winter at Fort Michilimackinac.

In the meantime, the Chippewa were so incensed that they showed up with their arms and threw their English belts into the lake, inviting other nations to join them in demanding the release of the major from his confinement. Once again, the natives were getting restless. On May 21, Rogers was transported by schooner first to Detroit, then to Niagara, and finally to Montreal. He arrived in Montreal on July 17, 1768; the trial did not begin until October 20, 1768. The evidence against Rogers was weak. He mounted an eloquent defense, and the court found him not guilty. He did go on to serve with distinction for the British during the Revolution. After the Revolution, his marriage fell apart, and he spent the rest of his life in obscurity.

In 1774, Maj. A. S. DePeyster took over the command at Fort Michilimackinac. In 1776, he was in command of English forces and all that were dependent on the fort for their livelihood as war with America had begun. In 1778, he was becoming concerned about reports of the American's plans to capture Fort Detroit and all British outposts on the

Northern Great Lakes. A letter was written and sent to General Haldimand on August 31, 1778. In the letter, he stated, "If Detroit should be taken we have but a dismal prospect." In October 1779, Captain Patrick Sinclair was named lieutenant governor and superintendent of affairs for the First Nations, in addition to his command of Fort Mackinaw. He arrived by boat from Detroit. On the way, he stopped at Mackinac Island. The retiring and incoming commanders compared the mainland and the island for military and defense purposes. Both agreed that the island offered the possible situation for the new fort. No time was lost in informing General Haldimand on the wisdom of moving the defenses to Mackinac Island. They received the approval of their joint recommendation that Fort Michilimackinac be removed from the mainland to Mackinac Island. There were at least two reasons for the urgency of the two British officers: the First Nations, who had remained hostile to the English, and the success of George Rogers Clark in the Ohio Valley. During the American Revolution, Clark and about 175 men marched to Kaskaskia (in present-day Illinois) and took the fort there on July 4, 1778, with no exchange of gunfire. Clark had also taken Fort Sackville at Vincennes (in present-day Indiana), but it was soon retaken by the British. Determined to regain the fort, Clark and about 170 men made a two-hundred-mile journey there—much of it through freezing floodwaters—in February 1779. At Vincennes, Clark managed to trick the fort's inhabitants into thinking he had a greater number of men with him. He demanded that the British commander, Henry Hamilton, unconditionally surrender. In order to show the Indian tribes in the area that their British allies could not protect them, and to intimidate Hamilton, Clark then ordered that four captured Indians be publicly tomahawked and killed. Hamilton agreed to nearly all of Clark's terms, where he had courageously defended the American frontier settlements from the British, particularly the scalp-buying English General Hamilton. He paid the Iroquois that were operating out at Fort Detroit for the scalps of dead Americans. Later he was captured as a prisoner and put into irons, then taken to Williamsburg, Virginia. There he was held until 1781, then shipped to New York for a prisoner exchange. With all this going on, there was a lot of anxiety on the leadership at Fort Michilimackinac.

Work parties were sent over to Mackinac Island at once to study the topography of the island. They reported the advantageous location rising nearly two hundred feet above the lake level and offering defense of the Straits. Another letter was written to General Haldimand, explaining that the position on Mackinac Island was probably the most respectable situation he ever saw. There was safety for the troops, traders, and commerce. He compared the position on Mackinac Island to his defenseless position on the mainland. Rock was readily available. However, the Island was an owned and occupied property of the First Nations. They really did not want to strain the relationship and indifferent attitude toward the English king by taking it by force. After some serious negotiations, a treaty was made with four chiefs. The terms of the treaty were that they sold forever the island of Michilimackinac for the cash sum of £5,000, or $25,000. This is the first known treaty in Michigan with the First Nations.

At this time, slowly but surely, the English trader was beginning to gain a foothold. Search for the peltries, like with the previous regime, was great business of the day, a business in which the almighty dollar beaver pelt let the First Nations enjoy their deserts in quiet. Were they driven from their forests, their peltry trade would decrease. This was a period of transition from French to English. They gained a firm foothold in Michigan. The trade subdued the First Nations and, to a certain extent, enlisted the British on their side against the coming enemy, the Americans.

Fort Mackinac (Island). During the winter of 1780–1781, the first structure to be moved across to Mackinac Island was the old Catholic Church. It was to be located in the lower village; the worship and work of the Canadians would be drawn to the island. There were difficulties in the tearing down, transporting, and reerecting the old buildings. Being a primitive construction delayed the work considerably. Projects began in 1780 and progressed slowly through that summer and into the winter of 1781. By July, Patrick Sinclair was able to report that all the troops and stores would be within the works of the fort by October 1781. All the remaining structures on the mainland were burned to the ground. So if the American rebels were to attack, they would not be able to use the fort in any way against the British. All the time the construction was taking place, they were keeping a watchful eye out for trouble, not only from the American rebels to the South, but also from the First Nations. No threat developed from either of the two enemies. The British now controlled the passage between three of the Great Lakes: Superior, Huron, and Michigan. There would be no navigational traffic passing through the South Channel, between Bois Blanc Island and the mainland for about another seventy years. Sometime around 1850, that was when there was navigational traffic passing through the South Channel. All navigational traffic to and from Lake Michigan had to pass through the North Channel, between Mackinac Island and Round Island.

During the Revolution, there was difficulty in shipping supplies in the years between 1780 and 1783. The British made steady progress on improving their position and defenses of the fort on the hill. In 1783, the

American Revolution came to an end with the signing of the Treaty of Paris. In those three years between 1780 and 1783, there was a major push to get the defenses of the fort completed. After the signing of the Treaty of Paris, they were unable to get the completion of the island fortress. Eventually, Captain Sinclair fell into disfavor with General Haldimand, largely because of heavy expenditures in which General Haldimand insisted that they were unnecessary. In 1782, the command at the new fortress was turned over to Capt. Daniel Robertson.

Long drawn-out disputes regarding the Canadian border line kept Fort Mackinac under the British flag for thirteen years after the Treaty of Paris. Naturally, the English were waiting to see whether their title would survive the territorial negotiations, and they were reluctant to expend time and money in further building. Also, it had been stipulated at the Treaty of Paris that the United States acknowledged that the Americans should be held accountable for the debts due British subjects, debts incurred before the war. But the young, new government of the US could not enforce the collection of these debts in opposition to statutes enacted by several states to defeat the British creditor. This failure of the American government to comply with one of the stipulations of the treaty gave the British a pretext for refusing to surrender the frontier posts, the retention of which kept the profitable fur trade in British hands, and the king maintained a toehold in the Ohio and Michigan Territories.

There was also this uncertainty as to its ownership. In 1784, Captain Robertson was succeeded by Lt.[3] George Clowes, followed in 1791 by Capt. Edward Charelton, who remained the commander until October 1796, when they lowered the English flag from the flagpole for the last time and turned the fort over to Maj. Henry Burbeck, the first American commander. Michigan was sending a representative to Ottawa, Ontario, Canada for about three years.

Before anything can be done be after the signing of the Jay Treaty, a lot of work would have to be done dealing with the First Nations; a treaty of peace had to be worked out: "The post of Michilimackinac, and all the land on the island on which that post stands, and the main land adjacent, on which the Indian title has been extinguished by gifts or grants, to the French or English Governments; and a piece of land on the main to the

---

[3] Abbreviated military commissioned officer rank

Lt. is short for *lieutenant*.

Capt. is short for *captain*.

Maj. is short for *major*.

Gen. is short for *general*.

Cmdr. is short for *commander*.

north of the island, to measure six miles, on Lake Huron, or the strait between Lakes Huron and Michigan, and to extend three miles back from the water of the lake or strait; and also, the island "Bois Blanc," The latter being an extra and voluntary gift of the Chippewa nation."[4] In October 1796, Maj. Henry Burbeck was in charge of two companies of United States soldiers. Along with Capt. Abner Prior, Lts. Ebenezer Massay and John Michael arrived and took possession of the post of Michilimackinac and completed the defenses of the island fortress. The British left Mackinac Island to Saint Joseph's Island and established a fort there. The officers at Fort Mackinac were aware of this fact and were determined more than ever to complete the fort. With all possible speed, the American occupation managed to finally complete the defenses of the fort. Capt. Abner Prior was commander of the fort until 1799.

---

[4]   "Annals of Fort Mackinac," language in article 13 of the treaty of peace between the US government and First Nations.

The War of 1812 at Fort Mackinac

Who won the War of 1812?
What three things did the war do for Canada?
What did the war do for the United States?
Where did the British get their ships for the Battle of Lake Erie?
Where did the Americans get their ships for the Battle of Lake Erie?
How did we get a fleet of ships on the Great Lakes to defeat the British?

Benjamin Franklin, upon receiving word of the signing of the Treaty of Paris, is quoted as saying, "War of Revolution was won, but the War for Independence is yet to be fought." Relations between the United States and Great Britain had been strained for some time now. One of the problems was the British boarding American vessels and impressing American sailors into service for the King of England. In 1811, the United States banned the importation of British goods. And also it was believed at that time that the British were encouraging the First Nations to attack the settlers on the frontier. This was the 1800's version of the Cold War. On June 18, 1812, war with Great Britain was declared by the Congress of the United States. By a vote of 79 to 40 in the House and 19 to 13 in the Senate, the House and the Senate declared war on Great Britain. On June 19, 1812, war was formally declared by President James Madison. In 1811, Lt. Porter Hanks took over command at Fort Mackinac, upon the death of Capt. Lewis Howard.

On July 16, 1812, the garrison at Fort Mackinac was blissfully unaware that war was declared since June 18, 1812. There were really only two ways of communication back then: one was by postal, and the other was by a carrier riding on horseback. The secretary of war for the United States preferred the postal medium for the communication to the frontier posts, informing them about the beginning of hostilities with Great Britain. It took fourteen days for the message to get to General Hull at Fort Detroit. It took the special messenger for General Brock four to five days sooner. Lt. Porter Hanks, at the island outpost on Mackinac Island, did not receive notification that hostilities began until it was too late. On July 8, Captain Brock officially notified Captain Roberts, the British commander at Saint Joseph Island, that he should act accordingly. Months before war was declared, the British were busily lining up additional help. On July 15, 1812, Captain Roberts received the orders from Brock. On July 16, 1812, due to the impatience of the First Nations, without hesitation, Captain Roberts decided to attack Fort Mackinac. On July 16, 1812, at Fort Mackinac, the soldiers were blissfully unaware that war had been declared. Lt. Porter Hanks was aware that something was amiss. The First Nations were more hostile than normal, and a lot of First Nations traffic headed up to Saint Joseph Island. With the information that he had, it was decided that Michael Dousman, because he was part of the island militia and was engaged in the fur trade, would have a legitimate reason for traveling to Saint Joseph Island. That evening on July 16, 1812, Michael Dousman was fifteen miles into his journey, when he encountered the British flotilla on its way to Mackinac Island.

He was taken prisoner and landed with the British at around 3:00 a.m. From British Landing, he went to town and rounded up the villagers where they were to go to the distillery and take refuge there, where they would be guarded by a British soldier. They were being protected from the First Nations. They would kill the villagers with them with no compunction. If they were to go to the fort for protection, their safety would be in jeopardy. Michael Dousman was not to leak intelligence to Lt. Porter Hanks at the fort about the British invading Mackinac Island. All the while, the British were emplacing a six-pound cannon on the heights overlooking the back of the fort.

While Dousman was evacuating the people of the village to the distillery, Dr. Sylvester Day, the post surgeon's mate, lived in the village; he ran breathlessly up the hill to the fort and told the post commander what was going on. Lieutenant Hanks made every conceivable preparation possible to meet an attack, calling out all fifty-seven men who were fit for duty that morning. As the men were assembling, Hanks was probably wishing at this point of being anywhere but where he was at that very moment. The fort was designed to survive small-scale attacks, nothing what the British had brought to bear on this day, certainly not from the north. Americans could have held out for a short period against the first wave. The source of water for the garrison was outside the fort, beyond the protection of the fort's guns. It was at this point that Lt. Porter Hanks realized that war had been declared, almost a month to the day after the fact.

Surrender was really the only solution to the problem. The British had the high ground. He was outnumbered, seventeen or sixteen to one. Their only source of water was outside the fort, with a six-pound cannon pointing at the most defenseless part of the fort. The gun boomed, and then a flag of truce went down with Roberts. Lieutenant Hanks was urged to surrender "in order to save the effusion of blood, which must of necessity follow the attack of such Troops." Hanks was given one-half hour to make up his mind. Accompanying the flag of truce came three Americans who had been taken prisoner to tell Lieutenant Hanks how useless it was to fight. The three were Samuel Abbott, John Dousman, and Ambrose Davenport. Probably the most profound quote of the war is "I was born in America and am determined at all hazards, to live and die an American citizen," the profound statement made by Ambrose Davenport. The islanders called his wife the Yankee Rebel. So you are left wondering about those who signed their allegiance to the Crown. What are they?

British Forces

Regular troops....................... 46 troops plus 4 officers

Canadian militia...................... 260 troops

Total................................. 306

First Nations

Sioux................................. 56

Winnebago............................. 48

Menominee.............................39

Chippewa and Odawa.................... 572

Total 715

First Nations 715

Militia and arm plus four officers 306

Total 1021

Americans

Sixty-three soldiers and officers, including five men who were on sick call and a drummer boy, Lt. Porter Hanks, were outnumbered from 16 to 1 or 17 to 1 with just the men who were healthy.[5]

Around noon, the terms of capitulation were signed. The fort was to be handed over to the British at once. The Americans would march out of the fort with the honors of war, lay down their arms, and become prisoners of war. The gentlemanly rules of war back then were that the Americans would be paroled and sent to American-held territory, with Lieutenant Hanks and his men pledging that none of the men would serve against the British until a regular exchange was made for British prisoners of war. The American citizens were given a month to sign their allegiance to the Crown. Those who did not had to leave. The colors were lowered; the Union Jack was flying above Fort Mackinac once again. The American prisoners were sent from Mackinac Island to Detroit, arriving there on August 4. Lieutenant Hanks was brought up on charges of dereliction of duty unbecoming an officer and cowardice for surrendering the fort. He was killed on August 16, while still on parole, by a shot fired from the Canadian side, while standing in his room at Fort Detroit. On that fateful day, the British seized all the ships that were docked when Fort Mackinac fell, including the *Salina* and two ships from Chicago. Later, at Fort Detroit, US Brigadier Adam was captured as well. The spoils of war went to the victors. In this case, the ships and their cargo went to the British.

Capt. Dan Dobbins was on his way to Fort Mackinac with a load of salt on his sailing ship, the *Salina*, when the fort was captured by the British. The British confiscated the ship and the load of salt. Capt. Dan Dobbins, with the help of some influential friends, negotiated his release and proceeded to Detroit. Detroit fell into the hands of the British; again he was able to gain release. From there, he headed to Cleveland, ultimately

---

[5]   From research, one source says it was sixty-one men and another source says sixty-three that were fit for duty on July 17, 1812.

making it to his home in Erie, Pennsylvania. He was afraid that Erie would suffer the same fate as Fort Mackinac and Fort Detroit. Dobbins reported his experience to General Meade, who was in charge of the state militia in Northwest Pennsylvania.[6] General Meade agreed that the American shore of Lake Erie was defenseless. Dobbins was advised to proceed to Washington, DC, and brief President Madison and his cabinet.

Dobbins had a unique set of qualifications for this particular mission. He had a reputation as the best seaman and navigator on Lake Erie. On his voyages on Lake Erie, he primarily carried whiskey, furs, and also home and food products. He really had no shipbuilding experience, though he did repair, overhaul, and maintain the ships he operated, including the *Salina*, which he was owner and master. Dobbins departed for Washington, DC, immediately, arriving around September 2 or 3, 1812. For about twelve or thirteen days, Dobbins was in a heated debate with the president and his cabinet members on the need for a navy on Lake Erie and the Great Lakes. On September 15, 1812, Dobbins was given authorization from the secretary of the navy to build four gunboats at Presque Isle on Lake Erie and was given $2,000 to get started. The following day, on September 16, he was appointed sailing master in the US Navy. The reason it was Erie, Pennsylvania, was the location, which included stands of large oak trees and forests that grew to the edge of the water. The peninsula of Presque Isle and the enclosed bay allowed for safe harbor with the entrance being protected by a sandbar with a depth of no more than six feet. Dobbins emphasized that ships could be constructed and be safe from raids or attacks from the British. When completed, the ships could be sallied over the sandbar into the deep water. Dan Dobbins was a good sailor and had no doubts that the ships could exit when built. Erie had an excellent safe harbor and an unlimited supply of timber.

The order was for four gunboats fifty feet in length, with seventeen-foot beam and a five-foot draft. The two brigs were sister ships, the *Lawrence* and *Niagara*, and were 118 feet in length. At the beam, they were thirty feet, and the draft on these boats loaded was nine feet. Everything had to be brought in by hand for the construction of the boats and ships. The paint, oil, iron, copper, guns, sails, ropes, cannon balls, and gunpowder— all would have to be moved over former trails made by the First Nations to Erie, Pennsylvania. Trees were paid for to the landowner at one dollar apiece. Due to lack of iron for nails, a large part of the hull was held together by wooden pins, or tree nails. There was a lack of oakum and pitch for caulking for all the seams and making the ships watertight, so

---

[6]   Gen. George Meade was born in 1815 and was also in charge of Union forces at Gettysburg during the Civil War.

lead caulking was used with great success. The green timber should have been seasoned for about one year. (When the *Niagara* was raised in 1913, one hundred years later, the lead caulking was still firmly in place.) The lead caulking of the green timber undoubtedly produced a watertight hull superior to oakum and pitch. The only large building available was the courthouse to cut, sew, and assemble the sails for the boats. The contracts for the iron, canvas, cordage, rigging, anchors, cannon balls, and other equipment were made in Pittsburgh. Of the shipment of the cannons for the boats, sixty-five of them in all, thirty-seven were from Washington, DC, made at the Foxall Foundry of George Foxall in Georgetown. The remainder was from Sackets Harbor. Fourteen wagons with four men each carried the carronades from Washington to Pittsburgh, requiring more than one month for the trip. Instead of using pig iron or stone for ballast for the ships, the shallow draft ships had insufficient space for the required amount of stone ballast, so Perry ordered lead to be used because it was readily available and because at any time, lead became necessary to resell.

The ships were framed and knocked together by woodsmen on the shores of Lake Erie. This was how the navy was built. In eight months, they built six boats along with five converted merchant ships: the *Somers*, *Trippe*, *Ohio*, *Caledonia*, and *Amelia*. This was the navy that kicked the British navy off the Great Lakes. The highest amount of skill was entered into the design and construction of the boats, and the citizens of the town of Erie, Pennsylvania, led by Dan Dobbins, had not ever received credit for their work of building six wooden ships of green timber in eight months. They were the American heroes of the War of 1812.

On September 10, 1813, by 2:15 p.m., the battle was over, with heavy casualties on both sides. All British ships were captured, and all the surviving officers and men were made prisoners of war. British losses numbered 41 dead, 94 wounded, and 306 captured. Barclay was wounded in the battle and was unable to participate at the end. American casualties were twenty-seven dead and ninety-six wounded. The *Niagara* was damaged in the battle. The *Lawrence* and *Niagara* would be able to be part of the expedition that attacked Mackinac Island. The captured pennants of the British ships were taken to Annapolis, Maryland, to be put on display. On September 29, America retook Fort Detroit from the British. All officers, with the exception of Dobbins, received a sword presented by Congress to all commissioned officers who participated in the battle.

Through the winter of 1813 and 1814, Captain Roberts got a debilitating stomach ailment and was relieved in command by Captain Bullock. On May 18, 1814, Col. Robert McDouall relieved Captain Bullock, bringing with him the Royal Newfoundland Regiment, provisions, and also about eighteen years' worth of experience in the British army. The British also made improvements to their position, digging a well inside the fort, improving the pickets and the fort on the heights overlooking the back of the fort, Fort George, named in honor of the British king, King George III. Later renamed Fort Holmes, it was completed in July of 1814.

The American naval operation to reclaim Fort Mackinac was being botched every step of the way, from beginning to the end. Capt. Arthur Sinclair of the US Navy was in charge of the operation. In the spring of 1814, there was a dispute in the high command over who was going to be in charge of the troops. Maj. Andrew Hunter Holmes was a distinguished officer from Virginia, assigned to the Twenty-Fourth US Infantry, who captured Jean and Pierre Lafitte and two dozen of their men. He was a pirate and running a slave ship. In March 1814, Captain Holmes and his company beat off a 240-man British column at the Battle of Logwoods in southern Ontario. The command of more than seven hundred men was given to Lt. Col. George Croghan from Kentucky, with Major Holmes being second in command, with five detached companies from the Seventeenth, Nineteenth, and Twenty-Fourth US Infantry and a battalion of volunteers from Ohio, along with a detachment of artillery.

They were not sailing directly to Mackinac Island. Mackinac Island was part of a more broad operation of disrupting the flow of supplies to Fort Mackinac and the fur trade with the First Nations. On July 3, 1814, they set sail through Lake Saint Clair and on into Lake Huron. They were looking for a place called Matchedash Bay. Not one person in the chain of command knew where this place was or how to get there. With there being no pilot or charts on board any of the ships and no one knowing their way around Georgian Bay, after several days, they decided to move on. Staying, they would risk hitting rocks or getting stuck on a submerged obstacle. Proceeding north up the Saint Mary's River to Saint Joseph Island, they burned the fort that was abandoned by the British. Out of that, they managed to capture schooners and other supplies. Major Holmes and a detachment of men ventured over land to Sault Sainte Marie; there they destroyed a stash of supplies for the British. After the raid, the operation turned its sights south on Mackinac Island.

The British had been expecting the Americans at any time, and on July 26, 1814, they sighted the Americans coming in from the east. Upon their arrival, they decided to anchor on the eastern end of Round Island. Shots from the British cannons from the fort were coming a little bit too close for comfort. They picked up anchor and withdrew back toward Bois Blanc Island. A party of men was sent to Round Island to scout and survey of possible positions for placement of the guns to cover the landing on the southern side of Mackinac Island. The scouting party was spotted; the men hastily beat it to their boats, and one poor soul was not fast enough and was captured by the First Nations. The British soldiers rescued the lucky soul, lucky in that the British were around to save his hide from the First Nations. This was their first chance to release pent-up emotions, and they wanted him. The next day, the *Lawrence* was exchanging fire with some British land-based cannons. Sinclair discovered the cannons on the ships could not be elevated high enough to be effective on the fort. So much for the attack from the front of the fort; none of the guns would be able to cover the landing.

After all this, any notion of an attack on the front side of the island was dismissed. Bad weather had moved in, hampering any further ambitions by the Americans. On the morning of August 4, nine days after their arrival in the Straits area, it all began. On the morning of August 4, 1814, Sinclair was about three hundred yards off British Landing, while the beach head was being swept with cannon fire, protecting the soldiers as they were sent to the beach. Colonel Croghan's immediate objective was an open field about a mile or so inland. Marines stayed back in reserve, and the rest of the force was to make their way to the Dousman farm. The British were not surprised at all by the movement of the Americans. Colonel McDouall was informed by spies as to what was happening with the Americans. He left a detachment of men at Fort Mackinac and at Fort George. The rest of the men, along with members of the First Nations, made their way to meet the enemy in the center of the island. Any hopes of the Americans establishing any kind of a foothold on the island were quickly dashed. At the Dousman farm were the thick woods, where members of the First Nations could conceal themselves and wait to ambush the unsuspecting Americans, with the four cannons that the British brought to bear on the Americans as well. At this point, there was no option for the Americans but to beat it out of there in retreat back to the ships. The expedition left the island with fifteen killed in action and about fifty or so wounded. Maj. Andrew Hunter Holmes, who at that point had a very distinguished career—he was second in command to Croghan—was killed on August 4, 1814. His remains were recovered and taken back to the ship. On the ship, his remains were placed in a wooden casket along with some cannon balls. If the British were to capture the ship, the casket was to be shoved overboard, where it would sink to the bottom of the lake.

The Americans still had one option that could bring the British at Fort Mackinac to their knees, and that was by cutting the remaining supply lines. The *Lawrence* and the *Caledonia* were sent to Detroit with the sick and the wounded, and the rest of the expedition set their course for Nottawasaga Bay. This was where the British were resupplying Fort Mackinac from. They found the bay, and then they headed up the Nottawasaga River for two miles. On August 14, 1814, the Americans destroyed the blockhouse that stored the supplies and the last remaining schooner for the British, the *Nancy*, which was loaded with supplies for Fort Mackinac. With their mission completed, Croghan and Sinclair, with the *Niagara*, set their course for Detroit, leaving the *Scorpion* and the *Tigress* to make sure that the supply lines to Fort Mackinac remained closed. On August 31, 1814, Lieutenant Worsley of the Royal Navy, who was in charge of the Nottawasaga base, escaped along with seventeen men and made it to Fort Mackinac. Along the way, he paid close attention to the location of the *Tigress* and the *Scorpion*, noticing that they were anchored in the area of Saint Joseph Island. The fort was on half rations, and the few horses that were on the island were killed and salted.

The British hatched a plan involving fifty members of the Newfoundland regiment, and several of the canoes were filled with members of the First Nations. On the first night, the expedition made it to Detour. On the night of September 3, 1814, while rowing the expedition, they finally spotted the *Tigress*. They were signaled by the Americans and were asked to identify themselves. The British made no reply, and the Americans opened fire on the expedition. Within five minutes, the British reached the American vessel, boarded her, and overpowered the crew of thirty men. They really had no chance to repel the boarding party. The British had two killed in action and seven wounded.

On September 5, 1814, the *Scorpion* was approaching the *Tigress*. The British stayed concealed by staying below deck or lying down on the deck so that they could not be seen. Worsley picked up anchor and set a course toward the *Scorpion*. While sailing toward the *Scorpion*, they signaled her using the signal book found on the *Tigress*. The British sailed to within ten yards of the *Scorpion*. It was too late for Commander Turner of the *Scorpion* before he even knew what was happening; the British quickly boarded the *Scorpion* and quickly seized control of the ship. The British now regained control of their supply lines with the capture of the *Tigress* and the *Scorpion*. The British all but secured the control over a vast area north of Detroit. The Union Jack remained flying high over the fort for the entirety of the war. Nothing but candor and admiration went to the British on their resourcefulness and ingenuity in the breaking of the blockade. With the inept leadership of the American expedition and the resourcefulness and ingenuity of the British, that was what really determined the outcome of the events.

December 24, 1814, was the signing of the Treaty of Ghent. The treaty provided that both sides were to relinquish all territory that had been conquered during the war. McDouall was not happy at all about the turn of events at the negotiations: "Our negotiators have been egregiously duped." Our negotiators were better than their negotiators. Finally, on July 18, 1815, three years and a day after Lt. Porter Hanks and his men surrendered to the British, Col. Anthony Butler, with troops of the Second US Regiment rifleman, relieved McDouall of the island, and once again the Stars and Stripes was flying over the fort. All the king's men were removed to Drummond Island. In 1822, with much dispute, Drummond Island was declared to be American soil. He was forced to leave and reestablish their fort at Saint Joseph's Island. This post was later on abandoned; the British influence was removed from the Mackinac Country forever.

Out of all this, there were winners and losers. Canada was the winner. Before 1812, many settlers, especially in what is now Ontario, did not feel particularly Canadian. Some were United States citizens who left the United States as Loyalists during the American Revolution. They were empire Loyalists, arriving to Canada after being driven north by the Revolution. Many others were more recent arrivals: they were Americans lured over the border by the prospect of easily available land. They really had no strong connection to Canada or the Crown of England. Collectively fighting for their land and seeing it ravaged by an invader, they went a long way in hammering these people into a unified whole—into *Canadians*. It solidified their allegiance to the British Crown, it gave them nationalism, it left Canada and its territory intact instead of being swallowed by the United States, and it laid the foundation for their future nationhood. To this extent, the Canadians were the real winners of the War of 1812.[7]

This was the war that gave us our identity, and in some ways, we have lost that identity. The outcome for the United States was not as obvious; the War of 1812 was the finale to the American Revolution. The War of 1812 firmly established our present northern border with Canada, with the outcome being the Battle of Lake Erie, which decisively determined the present-day boundaries on Lakes Erie, Huron, and Superior and westward. The British at one time had intent of the Ohio River westward to the Mississippi River as being the borders for a separate state for the First Nations. The outlook for the British Empire for North America was destroyed after the War of 1812. The British's hopes for their empire in North America were starting to diminish in 1803 with the Louisiana Purchase by President Thomas Jefferson from Spain. It gave us the full recognition and respect of the world for our rights and privileges as a sovereign nation. It also would end the British claim to certain territories in our country and the withdrawal of British troops from these territories.[8] We were very lucky to escape this war the way we did and take the British army to a draw. The British at that time were fighting us and were also fighting the French over in the European theater in the Napoleonic Wars. This could have had a very different outcome for both the United States and Great Britain. Now in the geopolitical world today, the United States and Great Britain are very strong allies. Today we share one of the longest open borders in the world and are friends with our Canadian friends to the north.

The only real losers in the War of 1812 were the indigenous people, or the First Nations. The first time that the First Nations were left high and dry by their British allies was at the negotiation of the Peace Treaty of 1783, at the end of the American Revolution. During the War of 1812, there were big differences in how the war was conducted. The First Nations' philosophy was basically to kill the enemy and save their people. They depended on stealth and spontaneous attack and did not understand the Europeans sustaining all those heavy casualties.

---

[7]   This information came from my course lecture notes from my Michigan history course at Saginaw Valley State University.

[8]   This information came from my course lecture notes from my Michigan history course at Saginaw Valley State University.

The British did try to negotiate a separate territory for the First Nations, but the Americans were standing firm and did not want it. It was a disappointing loss for the First Nations; they were never able to recover their lost territory. In the United States, they were steadily being removed from their traditional lands. Most infamous of these removals is the Trail of Tears. The Indian Removal Act of 1830 involved the Cherokee, Chickasaw, Choctaw, Muscogee, and Seminole (sometimes collectively referred to as the Five Civilized Tribes). There were numerous deaths from hunger, exposure, and disease along the way. In Canada, it was no different. They were being outnumbered in their own land, and what was forgotten in Canada was that if it were not for the First Nations, Upper Canada might have fallen. There were First Nation warriors fighting for both sides, not just for the British.

After the War of 1812, Fort Mackinac remained an active duty post until 1890. Between 1815 and 1895, there were many officers who served at Fort Mackinac as lieutenants, and some of these young officers would go on and attain high ranks in the army. They would go on to distinguish themselves in active service in the Civil War for both sides, the Union and the Confederate and the Spanish American War in 1898.

1827 Gen. Edwin V. Sumner, Second Lieutenant, Second Infantry

1827 Gen. Samuel T. Heintzelman, Second Lieutenant

1829 Gen. Kirby Smith, Second Lieutenant

1834 Gen. Jesse H. Leavenworth, Second Lieutenant, Second Infantry

1840 Gen. John C. Pemberton, Second Lieutenant, Fourth Artillery (He was born in Philadelphia, Pennsylvania. In 1814, after the Mexican War, Pemberton married a Virginian; her name was Martha Thompson. At the start of the American Civil War in 1861, Pemberton chose to resign his commission in the Union army and joined the Confederate army, despite his birth in the North and the fact that his two younger brothers both fought for the Union army. He resigned his commission, effective April 29. His decision was due to the influence of his Virginia-born wife. He did surrender Vicksburg to Grant on July 9, 1863. His nephew John is credited for inventing Coca-Cola.)

1845 Gen. Silas Casey, Captain, Second Infantry

1845 Gen. Fred Steele, Second Lieutenant (A western army post was later named in his honor.)

1852 Gen. George Meade, Captain, Topographical Engineer (During the survey of the Great Lakes, at one point, Lt. Orlando Poe was under Meade's supervision.)

From 1850 to 1895, the island was run as the nation's second national park by the United States Army, it was known as Mackinac Island National Park. After 1895, there was no longer a garrison at Fort Mackinac. The United States government transferred the national park over to the state of Michigan. Since 1895, it has been a state park. It is Michigan's first and oldest state park. Eighty-two percent of the island is owned and operated by the state park. As you approach to the right of the Grand Hotel, it sits on the bluff like an old European castle with a commanding view for all to see. The fort as a fortification seems to be a mixture of American frontier post and old-world castle. The thick walls and sally ports, bastions, and ditch, its four old blockhouses of logs, the powder magazines located near the east sally port, loopholes for muskets, sloping path down to the village, buttressed along the hillside with heavy masonry—all these make it sort of a mountain fortress. I found this quote from George Catlin; he was probably the one responsible for the national park concept here in the United States, and it is generally credited to the artist George Catlin. On a trip to the Dakotas in 1832, he worried about the impact of America's westward expansion on Indian civilization, wildlife, and wilderness. "What a beautiful and thrilling specimen for America to preserve and hold up to the view of her refined citizens and the world, in future ages! It is A Nation's Park; containing man, and beast, in all the wild and freshness of their nature's beauty!"

THE OTHER SEASON

Some are probably wondering what I am talking about. Believe it or not, there are two seasons to Mackinac Island, the tourist season and the other season. The other season starts around Labor Day and goes through Memorial Day weekend. The last of the workers and horses leave usually around the end of October. This is when Star Line and Shepler's ferry services end, and the only one that is running is Arnold Line. If you have the distinction or privilege to stay until the bitter end, more than likely you will be going across on Arnold Line. The other two will have stopped running the last Sunday in October. That has since changed. All three ferries run until the end of October. Once in a while, I will get lucky, and sometimes the barnmen will need help taking the horses to the boat, and I go with them on the horse boat. It does not cost me anything except for the time it takes to get over to Saint Ignace to help unload the horses and help put them into the trailer, and I ride for free, but you have to be willing to work.

We do not keep all the horses on Mackinac Island. The horses are taken off the island to a place forty-five miles north of Mackinac Island called Pickford. It is easier and cheaper for the company to ship the horses to the food than shipping the food to the horses. Twelve to eighteen horses stay through the winter for the taxis and the drays needed. I actually enjoy doing it. At this point, I will load my car and head for Alpena to see some of my aunts and one uncle that live there. Spending the day visiting with my aunts and uncle is one of those things I enjoy doing as I pass through Alpena, and then I head for Hemlock. On Mackinac Island, life settles down after a busy season.

At this point, the Arnold Line boat is running four times a day. The first weekend in December, Mackinac Island holds its Christmas bazaar. This is when they light the island Christmas tree. If there is snow on the ground, the ski season will begin. You can also snowshoe. About 82 percent of the island is state park, and a lot of it closed to snowmobiles. If you stay on the island during the winter, you can rent cross-country skis, and snowshoes rentals are available from the Balsam Shop (phone number 906-847-3591). Those places that are open in the off-season are Doud's Market, Alfred's, Patrick Sinclair's Bar, Mustang Lounge, Village Inn, Pontiac Lodge, the Bogan Lane Inn, and an assortment of bed and breakfasts. Christmas is over, and then we have New Year's Eve. The first week in January, the boat will stop running until the harbor ice leaves. In January, the island celebrates; Martin Luther King Day is observed, boats stop running, and the ice bridge forms.

After the boats stop running the first week in January due mainly to harbor ice, the island residents hope for an ice bridge. To get an ice bridge, you need approximately two weeks of zero-degree temperatures with no wind. Then you need some volunteers to go out and spud the ice, checking the thickness and safety of the ice. They will plant Christmas trees a certain distance apart. When the weather is bad, you can travel from Christmas tree to Christmas tree, making it safely across the ice. The Christmas trees are gathered up after Christmas and taken out to British Landing where they will sit until they are needed for the ice bridge. The day that it is safe to cross the ice is Freedom Day on Mackinac Island,

Freedom Day in the sense that they no longer have to depend on anybody to get across to the mainland. The bridge will last anywhere from two days to two months depending on the winter. Sometimes they do not get to have an ice bridge; they are the long winters.

Jason St. Onge is a firefighter for MIFD. He is one of three charged with the task and responsibility to check the ice. What needs to be said here is *no ice is safe ice*. It is a matter of physics. A certain amount of ice will support a certain amount of weight. They do not just fly across the ice. When the ice is not as thick as they think it should be to hold them, they will turn around and go back. After the ice is determined to be safe, the people checking the thickness and safety of the ice will walk the whole way with steel spuds to check the thickness of the ice every ten to twelve feet by chopping through the ice until they hit water. This is a slow process, and that is why it takes over two hours to walk three miles. After they get a ways (say two hundred yards), they will walk back to get their snowmobiles and bring them up to that point. *Do not ride out on ice that has not been checked.*

When to go? Well, the chests do not get puffed up and just head out on the ice. They pay attention to the weather reports, monitoring the currents, keeping an eye on the winds. There is hard ice (black), soft ice, slushy ice, and snow ice. What you want, ideally, is the clear black ice. It is void of air bubbles, unlike the white ice, or the snow ice, which is snow that has been blown into the water and frozen. Certainly, they take looks from above and ask friends who have flown how it looks. Ultimately, the only way to check the ice is to chop a hole in it and see how thick it is.

The other thing that you have to watch for is ice being blown out by the wind and the current. Sometimes the current can be calm, and the wind is blowing like dickens. There are times when the current is going fast and the wind is calm. You can check the current by cutting a hole in the ice, pushing snow in, and watching how fast and what direction it is flowing. Snow is an insulator, if there is snow on the ice, insulating the ice from the cold air.

The whole point is that this is not a tourist attraction. It should not be treated as something that you always wanted to do. The only certainty is uncertainty once the ice bridge is in. The locals and islanders know whom to ask about ice conditions and how the current is treating it. Many tourists come up see the trees and head out. They have no clue as to what lies ahead. Ask authorities if you do not know the conditions of the ice. Islanders do it for the freedom from a boat schedule and an airplane schedule. Remember, *no ice is safe ice*.

The ice bridge is important to the island, more important than just getting to the mainland. It allows the day trippers to come over and visit and spend their money. There is a twenty miles per hour speed limit, and helmets need to be worn on the island for snowmobiles. What is there to do on the island if you were to visit? There are lodges available if you are planning for an extended stay, and for the famished traveler, pubs and eateries play an important part in your dining experience. Contact the Mackinac Island Tourism Bureau for specific information.

If there is no ice bridge, there are only two different types of transportation getting to and from Mackinac Island. One is by airplane. The easiest way to get to Mackinac Island by plane is to go to Mackinac County Airport in Saint Ignace. For forty-eight dollars, one can catch a two-way flight over to Mackinac Island. Flights leave on a regular basis. Before you get to the airport, you should call to have the cab at the airport, if you will need transportation to town. In the off-season, the cab runs only when it is needed. After the luggage is loaded, you will get in the plane, and you will also get a once-in-a-lifetime chance to be copilot. It is a very short trip, but what an awesome view of the island. In six or seven minutes, it is over. The plane schedule is pretty much consistent throughout the year.

The other way is by boat. During the season, the boat leaves every half hour until Labor Day. After Labor Day, they gradually cut back the schedule. After the last Sunday in October, Star line and Shepler will stop running. Arnold Line is still running the Catamaran on a reduced schedule, Starline and Shepler's is also running on a reduced schedule as well. Later they will put the Cats away for the winter. The Huron is used for the winter until sometime in January, when the boat will stop running until spring. If the weather is cooperating, there is no harbor ice and the boat runs year round. Riding the plane or boat, you learn to make every trip count. Because you are not going across every day; you learn to make the most of every trip.

I am usually touching base with the company as to around what time they want me to show up for work. As you can see, there is a lot to see and do in the off-season. The trails in the state park are kept peaceful for the cross-country skiers and the snowshoeing. This is your chance to see the island for what it really is—all about the peace, quiet, and tranquility.

One of the most important things is groceries. There is a grocery store on the island, called Doud's Market. It is Michigan's oldest family-owned grocery store. It has been in the same family for about 124 years. If you do go in there, it looks more like a general store than a grocery store. It has a few staples, deli, dairy, and some liquor. Basically, if you forget something on the shopping trip, they have it. If you want to do the power shopping, you have to go across to the mainland to do so. In the winter, the island residents have only three ways to go grocery shopping; one is by airplane. The pilot charges forty-eight dollars round trip and by the pound for the groceries. To use the snowmobile as the grocery getter, you need the ice bridge. If there is no ice bridge, or the island residents have the US Coast Guard philosophy on ice—"No ice is safe ice—and do not like to fly, what they can do is call over to Glenn's Market in Saint Ignace, talk to the manager, and give him the order and credit card number. The order will be filled, charged to the credit card, taken to the airport, and flown across, and by the end of the day, it will be at your doorstep.

December

Christmas bazaar and lighting of the Christmas tree

Cross-country ski and snowshoe season begins (depending on snow).

Cozy accommodations and winter retreat packages are available.

New Year's Eve celebration

Monday is Euchre Night at the Mustang Lounge.

Tuesday is Trivia Night at the Mustang Lounge.

January

Cross-country ski and snowshoe season begins (depending on snow).

The boat stops running.

Monday is Euchre Night at the Mustang Lounge.

Tuesday is Trivia Night at the Mustang Lounge.

February

Cross-country ski and snowshoe season begins (depending on snow).

The island celebrates Mackinac Island Recreation Department's winter fest, cross-country ski/walk postcard, poker rally, ice stone-skipping contest, chili cook-off, and the Village Inn Winter Fest.

Monday is Euchre Night at Mustang Lounge.

Tuesday is Trivia Night at the Mustang Lounge.

March

The island celebrates Sainte Anne's and Saint Patrick's Day celebration. The island is starting to reflect on the new season that is just around the corner.

The company is contacting employees on when to show up to begin work.

Monday is Euchre Night at the Mustang Lounge.

Tuesday is Trivia Night at the Mustang Lounge.

APRIL

This is the month that the boats will start to run. In the middle of the month, some of the company employees will start to show up. There is a lot of work that has to be done before the horses can arrive. They will be opening up the barns and pulling carriages out of the barn, where they were stored for the winter. Water in the barns has to be turned on, floors in the stalls have to be replaced, and hay and oats have to start coming in. Getting the barns ready to receive the horses is a lot of hard work. The horses spent the winter in the Pickford area, about twenty miles south of Sault Sainte Marie, Michigan.

30/10/2006

While the barns are being readied for the horses on Mackinac Island, downstate I am getting my personal affairs in order, changing the address for all my bills and VFW and American Legion memberships taken care of. If it is an election year, I will fill out an application for an absentee ballot. It is almost like a major deployment for a military operation. I am usually starting to want to be at work. The company usually has me arriving around the twentieth of April. Most of the barnmen are glad when I arrive, because that means they do not have to do tours and I can help repairing stalls or whatever needs to be done in the barns. When I am at about Gaylord, which is an hour out of Saint Ignace, I will call to see if a load of horses is coming across. If there is, I will help take some up the hill. It is one less person they have to send down the hill. Also I can ride for free on the boat. If not, I will just do my thing, take my stuff to my room, and start moving in for the season.

THE GRAND HOTEL

How long is the famous front porch?
How many board feet did it take to build the original Grand Hotel?
How long was it supposed to take to build the original Grand Hotel?
How long did it take to build the Grand Hotel?
When did the Grand Hotel open?

In the beginning, we had the glaciers come scratching through. After the glaciers, we had the glacial lakes Algonquin and Nipissing. Glacial lakes were followed by the First Nations, a.k.a. Native Americans. The First Nations were followed by the first white man, the French. The fur traders, the missionaries, and the French were followed by the British. After the British left, the Americans showed up. The fur trade was king on the island until about 1834, when it moved west with the expansion of the country. The fishing industry flourished for a while, and then the bottom fell out. During the Victorian era, the wealthy wanted out of the hot, stifling, and stuffy cities during the summer. Mackinac Island was becoming a destination for the wealthy. It was also known for its candy. After WWI, fudge became the popular confection. With almost sixteen fudge shops, they can sell about a thousand pounds a day. In 1850, Mackinac Island became the nation's second national park. The making of Mackinac Island as a national park really brought the tourists in; now they needed a place to stay while on the island.

In 1871, Gurdon Hubbard lost some of his fortune to the Great Chicago Fire. About the only thing he had remaining of his fortune was about eighty acres he purchased on Mackinac Island. Today it is known as Hubbard's Annex. He subdivided the property and developed the property. He was probably the island's first developer. He had more desires than just the cottage community in the Annex; he wanted a hotel in the Annex, and the hotel would have been for the guests of the cottage community. The dream would never come to being. While he was on Mackinac Island,

Gurdon Hubbard developed a relationship with Francis B. Stockbridge. He also wanted a hotel, but not in the Annex. Stockbridge was being loyal to his neighbors.

Like his friend, Francis Stockbridge was a self-made man; he was a shaker and a mover. Stockbridge purchased a large tract of private land far removed from the Annex. Stockbridge bought the land for the new hotel. It was private property, the ground on which the Grand Hotel now stands. Stockbridge was always well aware of his limitations. He neither wanted to build the hotel himself nor run it. Stockbridge had the vision. He waited for others with the unique talents for the job to implement that vision. Numerous people did come forward to sponsor the concept of the new hotel; among them was George Pullman of the Pullman Rail Car Company. He was pioneer of the sleeping car (Pullman car). The Pullman Company rented sleeping cars; they never sold them. Stockbridge thought that Pullman's idea was a bit too modest. Stockbridge wanted a big hotel. Right at the moment when Stockbridge's vision was starting to come together, Stockbridge found a higher calling; he was leaving the Michigan State Legislature to become a US senator in Washington, DC. Someone else would have to take up his vision for a big hotel on Mackinac Island. Stockbridge sold his hotel site to three transportation companies, with a great need to move their customers to resort areas by land and lake. The conglomerate was made up of the Grand Rapids and Indiana Railroad, the Michigan Central Railroad, and the Detroit and Cleveland Steamship Navigation Company. Each company had one-third share in the company's new stock. The company's name was called the Mackinac Island Hotel Company.

The Grand Rapids and Indiana Railroad was often referred to as the Fishing Line for bringing wealthy anglers to Northern Michigan. It had a lot to do with the clean, crisp air. It was also probably responsible for putting Petoskey, Michigan, on the map. In 1882, it pushed through to Mackinaw City as well. That was where that railroad ended. The Michigan Central Railroad went from Buffalo to Detroit to Chicago. In essence, it was part of the New York Central Railroad. The New York Central was everything east of Buffalo, New York. It was owned by Cornelius Vanderbilt, also known as the Commodore. The Michigan Central was the prime line for the state of Michigan. Its first passenger train to the far north from Detroit reached Mackinaw City in 1881. By 1882, it was possible for people in the leading cities in the Midwest to reach Mackinaw City in roughly a day's worth of travel.

The Detroit and Cleveland Steamship Navigation Company, the name is self-explanatory. For those going north from Cleveland and Detroit, particularly those less hurried customers who wanted to avoid the heat and dust of the trains, this was the perfect trip. The Detroit and Cleveland began its service to Mackinac Island in 1882. The next year, they launched their three-hundred-foot Mackinaw City, which steamed north from Detroit in thirty hours. These three transportation companies had a vested interest in the tourism and transportation of summer visitors.

In 1884, the Grand Rapids and Indiana Railroad had to admit frankly that Mackinac Island's hotels were overcrowded and that as to quality, there was little choice between them. The dilemma could be summed up like this: all dressed up and no (comfortable) place to go. The decision to build the Grand Hotel in 1886 by the three transportation companies was practical. What the three companies were looking for was a building, a place, a hotel that could advertise itself as the *ultimate destination*. The hotel had to be built first. The Mackinac Island Hotel Company commissioned Charles W. Caskey, an architect builder, to use the design plans from Mason and Rice of Detroit. Actually, the Mackinac Island Hotel Company put out a contract to have the Grand Hotel built in 1886. It would make the contractor a pretty wealthy man, and somewhat the conditions of the contract were pretty unreasonable. They wanted the hotel up and running for the season in 1887. No one was interested in the project. The only way it could be pulled off was that the materials had to be brought over in the fall of 1886; the supplies would spend the winter on the island. In the spring, the work gangs would arrive and have at it and start the construction. They had to build a two-hundred-guest hotel in around ninety days. They had to have it opened and running. Most contractors did not want to have anything to do with it.

The only builder to bid on the project was Charles W. Caskey. He was a burly and confident man; he was a builder from downstate. In 1880, he went north and built a summer home for himself in Harbor Springs. That was where he settled down and started to receive building commissions from wealthy people on Mackinac Island; a significant number of those came from the Annex. In a short period, Caskey had become a famous builder of solid and beautiful homes. To build the hotel, Caskey had to put aside a season of building summer homes. The contract for the Grand Hotel would more than make up for that when he completed it. Caskey opened up his own sawmill over in Saint Ignace. The fall of 1886 was wet and with lots of rain. That made it hard to get the lumber from the woods to the sawmill. Hardly any supplies made it over to the island that fall. Caskey needed a hard, cold winter to ferry the lumber and other building supplies to the island for the Grand Hotel project come springtime. Horse-drawn sleighs were hauling the lumber and other supplies across the four-mile stretch of ice bridge to Mackinac Island. They could not use the pasture for the fort, which is now the Jewel, the front nine for the Grand Hotel golf course. They used the land that is now the Tea Garden. Several piles of lumber turned into one monstrosity of a lumber pile that could be seen in Mackinaw City. They ran out of room for separate piles, so there was nowhere to go but up. People were traveling to Mackinaw City to see a lumber pile. Try to imagine about 1,500,000 feet of lumber piled and having guys working with ropes and pulleys, stacking the lumber. Windows, doorknobs, hinges, roofing, nails, screws, even locks and keys for the doors and a key-making machine—everything to build the hotel was brought over that winter. And he got it over there too.

In the spring of 1887, he hired a steamboat to bring over the work crews, the finishing wood, window glass, and all the tools. The post commander at Fort Mackinac would not allow the lumber to be placed in the pasture, but he would allow the workers to sleep there though. After arrival, some of the workers decided to strike for higher wages. Caskey needed the workers for the completion of the project; Caskey was direct: "I have to finish this job by a specified time for specified amount of dollars. My contract with you is legal and fair, and you knew that full well, together with my terms and needs, when you signed on. If you strike, my responsibility for your comfort and safety on Mackinac Island ceases. My boat will not make a special trip back to the mainland for you. If you strike, you are stuck on the island—without a job, without any money." Whether they realized it or not, in the end Caskey needed the workers to complete the project and the workers needed Caskey for the job. It is kind of like the relationship today, with the island depending on the hotel for tourists and the hotel depending on the island for the destination. This was a symbiotic relationship where both parties depended on the other. Construction of the hotel in the hand of the average builder would have taken two summers. Caskey, using six hundred workers, three shifts, and 1,500,000 feet of lumber, finished the job in ninety-three days.

To do this, they could not wait for the foundation to set up. They had to build after they poured the concrete. There were no nail guns, no power saws, no electric lights; everything was done by hand and by candlelight. Close had to be close enough, because you really had to keep moving on the project, especially with the lack of light. It was easier to shore it up than to try to make it plumb. Walking upstairs that creaked, walking down a hallway that was not quite plumb, and the rooms that were not quite square—these actually added to the charm of the Grand Hotel. In the beginning, the guests would stay for the season and would leave some of their belongings that they did not need over winter. The belongings would be waiting for the guests when they returned. When they came, it was not suitcases; it was two or three trunks full of stuff. Basically, they brought everything but the kitchen sink and then some. They also brought carriages; these would winter over and were kept in the Grand Stables. In the spring they were greased and ready to go for the season.

When they opened, they offered a clean new hotel. They had the only working elevator in the region at that time. Victorians were romantics, and that was what they were looking for when they came to the Grand Hotel. It was completed July 7, 1887. The Grand Hotel's front porch is iconic; it was and is today the world's longest front porch. It started out at 440 feet long, expanded to 626 feet, and now currently is 660 feet in length.

Now we welcome our first owner, John Oliver Plank. He was an investor in the hotel. He was manager from 1887 to 1890. His running of the hotel was not bad; he ran an efficient hotel but was really missing what the people of that time were looking for. They were looking for more than just good lodging, good food, and a pretty place.

After the departure of Plank, we bring in James Reddington Hayes. He arrived as manager of the Grand Hotel. He served as manager from 1890 to 1900. He got it right. His nickname was the Comet. He blazed from one property to the next. He wanted to give the guests something to do, more than lodging. He brought music to the Grand Hotel, live quality music. Day or night there was to be music playing somewhere in the hotel. It was all about the guest. He started the daily schedule of events. It is still used today. He also brought conventional tennis and baseball, and he blazed unconventional sports, like greased-pole climbs, carrying eggs on a spoon, stuff like that. He gave the hotel something more than just good lodging and food. He gave it a heart and a soul. He turned the hotel into a destination in itself.

Henry Weaver was the hotel's next manager. He served as manager from 1900 to 1910. He was from Saint Louis, Missouri. He kept many of the traditions alive. Halfway through his lease in 1905, he went to the Mackinac Island Hotel Company and threatened not to open the hotel. He made them a proposal; he said, "Give me half the stock in the Mackinac Island Hotel Company. Allow me to purchase the second half of the stock with my lease payments from 1905 to 1910. In 1910, I will be the sole owner of the Grand Hotel. You will still have a destination for your train guests and your steamship guests." They went for it, because that was their goal all along. He made changes to pricing and added amenities. In 1910, he broke trust with the island and announced that he was going to tear down the hotel. The Grand Hotel and Mackinac Island have a symbiotic relationship. Each place benefits from the other or needs the other. He felt he could get more for the lumber than he could ever get from the lodging. The island rallied, saying, "We need to have the Grand Hotel, put the hotel up for sale and we will work to find a buyer." He agreed to do that, and from 1910 to 1918, the Grand Hotel was for sale.

J. Logan Ballard served as manager of the hotel from 1918 to 1923. Islands are great places to run remote gambling operations. We were into the roaring '20s, with Prohibition and the whole nine yards. J. Logan Ballard passed away in 1923. The Ballards were unsure whether or not the hotel would remain open. The island was encouraging the family to keep it open. They interviewed for the manager position. Mr. Woodfill learned all the different departments of the house by working in them all. As he was working his way up in the hotel, Mr. Ballard passed away. He was used in the interview because he had worked in all the departments and could answer all the questions. In 1925, Mr. Woodfill went from front desk to manager.

W. Stewart Woodfill served as manager from 1925 to 1929. They needed to look prosperous to be prosperous. The Grand Hotel was starting to reflect its age, becoming worn and dated, and Mr. Woodfill decided they needed some upgrades. That was going to take a great deal of money. They sold part of the business to avoid additional loans. They sold one-third of the business to night auditor Eugene La Chance and another one-third to Mr. Woodfill. With that cash that he now had, he went to Chicago, needing more money, going to bank after bank, getting thrown out of just about every bank he visited. Lake State Bank was his last hope. The banker gave Mr. Woodfill the money. He renovated and made improvements to the Grand Hotel, but it needed much more work.

During Prohibition, there was not a dry day at the Grand Hotel. The booze flowed better than water did from the pipes at the Grand Hotel. Conveniently located fifty-two miles from Canada, coaches would meet boats on the other side of the island in the middle of the night and bring the booze back to the hotel. Gaming tables and gambling were where the money was to be made. Mr. Ballard had put in a secret room; it was called the Brighten Pavilion. It had a secret hallway and a door with a little panel that would open, and a pair of eyeballs would appear, just like in the movies. You had to have a card from the Grand Hotel Gaming Society to be allowed in. It was a speakeasy with blackjack tables, dancing girls, and the whole nine yards. It had a stage and a bar, where the liquor flowed into the wee hours of the morning. Roulette wheels were highly valued. If raided, the Roulette wheels would and up at the demise of the fire axe. They were very difficult to get and expensive to replace. These were placed in two more secret rooms. The rooms were raised and placed on ball bearings with fake walls. If raided, they would push on the wall. It would turn, and the roulette tables and gamers would disappear. An old lady would appear in a rocking chair, knitting. The raiders would leave, and the roulette tables and gamers would resume their fun.

In 1927, W. Stewart Woodfill knew what his one-third was really worth and asked his partners to buy him out; they bought his interests. His partners thought the prosperity of the roaring twenties was never going to end. Whether or not Woodfill knew what was coming, it was a very smart move on his part. They gave him a large amount of cash they had on hand, enough to pay off his loan and put the rest in the bank. They could not pay the note off; they gave him a nice monthly check.

In October 1929, the bottom fell out of the market. Bankers took over the Grand Hotel and ran it under the guise of receivership. The bankers brought in the best people they knew who were the best at running hotels. They could not sell the property for anything; it never made a profit. The only way for a return was to rent rooms. In the end, they basically surrendered. They found out what everybody else before them already knew, that is, the Grand Hotel did not turn a profit. The verdict was that the big hotel lost money every day.

In 1933, the bank put the hotel up for public auction. The auction was in the wintertime and had to be held on the property. The man with the papers came across on sleigh; W. Stewart Woodfill came across on a sleigh to purchase the Grand Hotel. It was probably the darkest day for the Grand Hotel, two months away from being demolished. W. Stewart Woodfill was very prudent and thrifty with his capital after the sale in 1927. This would put him in a position of being the sole bidder of the Grand Hotel at the auction.

W. Stewart Woodfill, in 1933 to 1979, was the sole owner of the Grand Hotel. From this day to the present, it has remained in the same family. He became the new owner of the Grand Hotel during the bleakest year of the Great Depression. He nurtured the Grand Hotel through the 1930s, even in 1939, when he had more on payroll than he had guests. They made it through the Great Depression, and they also made it through to survive WWII. They made it through the trying times with their chin up, dusting themselves off and marching forward. The building of the whole hotel took ninety-three days to build. The building of the presidential suite and the governor's suite took two years. They did not have the furniture for either of the suites. They went to purchase some furniture, and there was no credit to be had. He had a piece of paper called the Furniture Plan. This piece of paper had instructions as to where to get the furniture if someone was to rent the presidential or governor's suite. Also when you turn the paper over, you'll find out where to return a specific piece of furniture and where it was to be placed.

In 1947, Hollywood came to the island with Esther Williams and Jimmy Durante in *This Time for Keeps*. It was a big hit and one of her many films about swimming. Today the Grand Hotel has the Esther Williams Suite, named after the actress. There is the Esther Williams Swimming Pool as well. In the movie, Grandmother's house is actually Corner Cottage, at the corner of Market and M-185. In 1951, the Grand Hotel made a profit after the doors are closed and the books are done.

In 1951, Dan Musser came to the Grand Hotel to work for his uncle W. Stewart Woodfill. On Dan Musser's first year, he was the assistant to the chef. The next two years, he was waiter in the main dining room while he was going to college. When he was finished with college, he asked his uncle for a job. W. Stewart Woodfill insisted that Dan Musser do what his uncle did. He was going to learn the hotel business inside and out, working all the departments, and when transferred, he had to work twice the hours for the first two weeks to show there is no favoritism. He would make a nice hotelman if he survived that. In 1960, he became manager of the Grand Hotel, and by 1961, he was president of the Grand Hotel.

In 1979, Hollywood came to Mackinac Island once again for *Somewhere in Time*, with Jane Seymour and Christopher Reeves and Christopher Plummer. It is believed to have the second-largest following of fans to *Gone with the Wind*. The Grand Hotel usually has a Somewhere in Time Weekend; it is usually around the third weekend in October. In 1979, W.

Stewart Woodfill put the hotel up for sale, and Dan and Amelia Musser purchased the Grand Hotel.

Dan Musser served as owner of the Grand Hotel from 1979 to 2011. The Mussers represent the next generation to be the stewards of the Grand Hotel. When they took over, the hotel was worn and dated. Money needed to be injected into the hotel to the standard that they wanted to achieve. They upgraded the wiring and the plumbing, realizing conventions were the future. They decorated some meeting rooms and hired a sale staff. The front porch was reinforced, and the building was structurally sound. They managed to do something that is very difficult to do, and that is, they tried to be best of many periods. You can see that as you walk around the Grand Hotel today.

In 1976, the Mussers hired Colton Varney to do the interior decorating at the Grand Hotel. Looking around, he saw the colors out in the gardens. Every color that you see out there in the garden will be going into the hotel. He banned the color beige at the Grand Hotel. Geranium is the hotel flower. Each of the 385 rooms is decorated differently. When you are at the Grand Hotel, it is your birthday. You have two packages or gifts to choose from: one is wrapped in plain brown paper with a string, and the other is wrapped in pink and striped paper with a bow and possibly some flowers. Which one will you pick? He was not decorating; he was gift wrapping a summer memory, because that is what the Grand Hotel sells.

In 1987, in preparation for its centennial season, the Cupola Bar was added, the Woodfill Conference Center was completed, and the Jewel golf course was renovated. In 1989, Dan Musser III became president of the Grand Hotel. Also in 1989, the East Wing was added to the Grand Hotel. In 1994, the Woods Nine opened, combining with the original Grand Nine to comprise the Jewel, Grand Hotel's eighteen-hole golf course. In 1998, five new named rooms in honor of former First Ladies Lady Bird Johnson, Betty Ford, Rosalynn Carter, Nancy Reagan, and Barbara Bush were added to the west end of the hotel. Two new two-bedroom suites, the Grand and the Carleton Varney, were also added to the west end. In 2011, Dan Musser stepped down and retired from running the Grand Hotel. His son Dan Musser III took over the day-to-day operations of the hotel. When it was first built, "the big hotel looked indigenous to the horizontal lines of the bluff on which it was built." The Grand Hotel belonged where it was.

The Grand Hotel has been owned or associated with the same family from 1919. Being owned solely by the same family from 1933 until present, the same family has run the hotel. They all had to work all the departments before ownership. The Grand Hotel is a living, working museum. The

Grand Hotel today still remains a destination in itself. The struggle to remain historical and to meet the demands of guests with modern amenities will always be there. If you do visit the Grand Hotel, even if it is just for the day, make sure you make it up to the Cupola Bar. It is one of the best views of the Straits area around. Each owner of the hotel brought along something that was needed to make the hotel relevant, and it is still being employed by the hotel today.

Some Facts about the Grand Hotel

Grand Hotel is not the oldest hotel on the island. The oldest hotel on the island is the Island House, built in 1852. The Island House Hotel has the distinction of being the only hotel located within the boundaries of the pristine Mackinac Island State Park.

Grand Hotel was built in 1887 in just over three months (ninety-three days) by six hundred workers.

Grand Hotel originally had two hundred rooms and now has 385 individually decorated guest rooms.

Five US presidents have stayed at the Grand Hotel: Presidents Clinton, Bush, Ford, Kennedy, and Truman.

Grand Luncheon Buffet is over one hundred feet long and has more than seventy-five different food items to choose from.

The Main Dining Room serves just over fifty thousand of the hotel's signature dessert, the Grand Pecan Ball.

The main dining room can seat over 1,200 people.

The swimming pool at the Grand Hotel was built in the late 1920s and not for Esther William's film *This Time for Keeps*. That film was twenty years later. The pool was later named in her honor after the movie's release in 1949. Esther Williams swam in the Grand Hotel pool every day during the summer filming of the movie. A hastily assembled submersible coal-fired heater was used to heat the pool.

The Esther Williams swimming pool holds 330,000 gallons of water and is just short of a football field length.

The Grand Hotel remains the largest seasonally operated resort hotel in the United States.

The Grand Hotel's front porch is the world's longest, at 660 feet long, with one hundred rocking chairs.

Grand Hotel rates are per person and include a full breakfast and a formal five-course dinner each day.

The Grand Hotel has a formal dress code after 6:00 p.m.: the gentlemen in coat and tie and the ladies in their finest, not necessarily a dress, but a nice pantsuit is acceptable.

The Grand Hotel restaurants are open to the public. Please call the hotel for information and reservations.

WEST BLUFF

The Mackinac Bridge. It probably always has been a dream or desire to somehow connect Michigan's Lower Peninsula and Upper Peninsula. There was this disconnect before the bridge was built. There was a sort of disconnect with the residents of the two peninsulas. Now it is due to the proximity to the state capitol, not geological. The only connection was a ferry service that would take and ferry the trucks and automobiles back and forth. Traffic heading to the Upper Peninsula could be backed up to Cheboygan, Michigan, and for miles for traffic heading to the Lower Peninsula. The American Bridge Company started construction in May 1954 and completed in November 1957. Dr. Steinman was the chief design engineer on the project. He was also guest speaker for the graduating class of 1975 at Michigan Tech University.

In 1934, Murray D. Van Wagoner was the Democratic state highway commissioner who insisted that the Michigan legislature establish the Mackinac Bridge Authority. In 1940, the bridge authority reported that building a bridge was feasible. A year later, the causeway for the north approach for the bridge was built. WWII came. In 1947, the Michigan Legislature abolished the Mackinac Bridge Authority. In 1948, G. Mennen Williams won the gubernatorial election. In 1950, he recommended the reestablishment of the Mackinac Bridge Authority. The legislation was enacted, but it limited the newly created authority to determine feasibility only. In January of 1951, the authority submitted a very favorable preliminary report stating that a bridge could be built and financed with revenue bonds for $86,000,000, but because of the shortage of materials due to the Korean outbreak, legislation to finance and build the structure was delayed until early in 1952. The governor, on April 30, 1952, signed into law Public Act 214, which was sped through the legislature. This act had immediate effect, authorizing the Mackinac Bridge Authority to bond, build, and operate a toll bridge. In 1952, the Bridge Authority was clear to sell bonds to raise money to build the bridge. Legal problems arose with the selling of the bonds. Legal issues got cleared up, and in May 1953, there was a ground-breaking ceremony in Saint Ignace. It almost looked like the bridge was not going to be built. Finally, after all those years of waiting, the bridge was going to be built.

The first construction challenge awaiting them was to establish precise locations for each of the thirty-four bridge support foundations. This was done by establishing eight land- and six sea-based surveying stations. From these positions, the surveyor utilized triangulation techniques to plot the exact position for each bridge section. While the surveying was taking place, one of the largest armadas of marine construction equipment was being assembled in the Straits area to begin construction on the Mackinac Bridge. Others had begun assembling the caissons and superstructures as far off as Indiana, Pennsylvania, and Ohio. Alpena, Michigan, was where some of the caissons were assembled. The construction of the foundation went to Merritt-Chapman & Scott Corporation. Piers 17 and 22, the huge anchorages for the cables (they used cofferdams), and piers 19 and 20, the support for the forty-six-story towers, were difficult to build. For the tower piers, huge caissons were filled gradually with rock and cement and lowered carefully to bedrock with precise calculation. Between the anchorage piers and the cable tower piers with two cables went piers 18 and 21. These two required huge foundations. On November 21, 1957 to 1998, it was the world's longest single-span suspension bridge. In the winter, work in the Straits ceased. On land, though, work on the individual sections of the bridge continued.

Winters in Northern Michigan can be brutal, sometimes not fit for man or beast. There was a project with a deadline to meet. Another plan for building a bridge across the Straits, which was the original plan to bridge the Straits, was to build a bridge from Cheboygan to Bois Blanc Island, build another bridge from Bois Blanc Island to Round Island, then build another bridge from Round Island to South edge of Mackinac Island, then from Mackinac Island to Saint Ignace. That is almost twenty-five miles long, five times the length of the Mackinac Bridge. On November 7, 1940, the Tacoma Narrows Bridge failed. It was also known as Galloping Gertie because of the up and down motion it would make when under wind stress. It was the wind stress that caused it to fail, or collapse. Three years after the Tacoma Narrows disaster, engineer David B. Steinman published a theoretical analysis of suspension-bridge stability problems. Among his recommendations were that future bridge designs include deep trusses to stiffen the bridge deck and an open-grid roadway to reduce its wind resistance. In January 1953, Steinman was appointed as the design engineer for the Mackinac Bridge, and his recommendations were incorporated into its design. The bridge represented a new level of aerodynamic stability in suspension bridges for its time. In the spring and summer, work would go on out in the Straits on the foundations, anchorages, towers, and stringing cable. In the winter, work would continue on the bridge sections. Sometimes in the winter, weather in the Straits area was not fit for man or beast. Winters can be very brutal in Northern Michigan. In a little over three years, it was completed. All-weather travel was now possible with the completion of the Mighty Mac.

The Golden Gate Bridge is longer between the two towers, but the Mackinac Bridge is longer in total length. The Mackinac Bridge is currently the third-longest suspension bridge in the world. In 1998, the Akashi Kaikyo Bridge in Japan became the longest, with a total suspension of 12,826 feet. The Great Belt Bridge in Halsskov-Sprogoe, Denmark, which also opened in 1998, is the second-longest suspension bridge in the world, with a total suspension of 8,921 feet.

The Mackinac Bridge is the longest suspension bridge in the Western Hemisphere. The length of the suspension bridge (including anchorages) is 8,614 feet. The length from cable bent pier to cable bent pier is 7,400 feet. The length of the main span (between towers) is 3,800 feet. The total length of the Mackinac Bridge is 26,372 feet. The steel superstructure will support one ton per lineal foot per roadway (northbound or southbound). The length of the steel superstructure is 19,243 feet. Each direction will, therefore, support 19,243 tons. The answer is 38,486 tons (2 × 19,243 tons). No workers were buried alive while pouring the concrete. If someone had fallen in, they would have been retrieved so as to not affect the integrity of those piers. Even if a wooden block was to have fallen in, it would have been retrieved.

Some Facts about the Mackinac Bridge

☐ Five men lost their lives building the Mackinac Bridge. The five men are memorialized on a plaque near the bridge's southern end.

☐ Diver Frank Pepper ascended too quickly from a depth of 140 feet on September 16, 1954. Despite being rushed to a decompression chamber, the forty-six-year-old died from the bends.

☐ Twenty-six-year-old James LeSarge lost his balance on October 10, 1954, and fell into a caisson. He fell forty feet and likely died of head injuries caused by impact with the crisscrossing steel beams inside the caisson.

☐ Albert Abbott died on October 25, 1954. The forty-year-old fell from four feet (1.2 meters) into the water while working on an eighteen-inch-wide (forty-six centimeters) beam. Witnesses speculate he suffered a heart attack.

☐ Twenty-eight-year-old Jack Baker and Robert Koppen died in a catwalk collapse near the north tower on June 6, 1956. Koppen's body was never recovered. For both, it was their first day on the job. All five men are memorialized on a plaque near the bridge's southern end. Contrary to folklore, no bodies are embedded in the concrete.

The cottages that I talk about in this book are the ones that have come up in conversation during my private tour. To cover all the cottages, I will be just be rewriting a book, and I have no desire to rewrite a book that is wonderfully written in the first place. The name of the book is *Historic Cottages of Mackinac Island*. These Cottages are on private property, and please treat them as such.

The Pines. The Pines was built for the John Cudahy's family. John's ability to take risks had something to do with his confident and ambitious personality. At one point, because of some risks that he took, he was completely wiped out of all assets, when he tried to corner the market in pork and lard and lost four million dollars in 1893. He regained his standing in the industry, recouping his losses with help from his brothers, and gained another fortune to boot. Brother Michael reconstructed LakeCliffe, and Brother Edward never built but later bought his brother's LakeCliffe Cottage. Patrick Jr. wrote, "Poverty has been the making of many prosperous men." Subsequent owners include Eugene McDonald, founder of Zenith Radio Corporation. He formed and was the first president of the National Association of Broadcasters and pioneered the development of the short-wave radio. When the United States entered World War I, he enlisted in the naval intelligence service and eventually became a lieutenant commander. He kept the title for the rest of his life. Mr. McDonald was married once but divorced in 1947. There were two children born to the marriage: Jean Marianne and Eugene McDonald Jr. The son was known as Stormy. And also six-term governor of Michigan G. Mennen "Soapy" Williams and his wife, Nancy, spent time here at the governor's summer residence as obligations of the office allowed. After final term in office, Nancy and Soapy bought the Pines Cottage, enjoying it for twenty five years. It is now owned by Richard and Jane Manoogian from Detroit. He owns MASCO Corporation, and they are the largest manufacturers of brand-name products for the home improvement and new home construction markets. They donated the Manoogian Mansion to the city of Detroit.

(Shingle style. The arched breezeway below the veranda diverts wind to cool all four levels of the cottage. The cottage is sheathed in wooden fish-scale shingles. The lattice brings the detail together to give a unified round and smooth appearance.)

White Pines. White Pines was owned by David and Margaret Hogg. David Hogg was from Kinross-shire, Scotland, in 1842. He was the son of Robert and Elizabeth (Scott) Hogg. Educated in his homeland like Hannah, Hogg emigrated in 1863. He worked as a painter and paper hanger in the eastern United States after arriving here and went to Chicago in 1869. There he worked for several years in the wallpaper business with two local firms. Then Hannah and Hogg met, and in June 1873, they formed a partnership to run a drinking establishment called the Thistle. Later on, they branched into the wholesale and retail liquor and cigar trade. The name on the brand was simply Hannah and Hogg. Hannah was president, and Hogg was vice president. They both married sisters. In the midst of all the enterprise, David Hogg met and married Margret Grady in 1875. They had four children. In Chicago, the two families lived within a block of each other on Oak Street. It is currently owned by Richard and Jane Manoogian from Detroit, who also own the Pines right next door.

Cairngorm. Cairngorm was owned by Alexander and Catherine Hannah. Hannah was born in Wigtownshire, Scotland, in 1845. He was the son of Alexander and Mary (Patterson) Hannah. Educated in the public schools of Scotland, at the age of twenty-three, he immigrated in 1868 to the United States. Upon arrival, he headed to the Midwest and found his first job as a clerk in Bernard, KA ("Hannah & Hogg Sowed Thistles in Chicago").

In 1872, he moved to Chicago, where he met fellow countryman David Hogg. The partnership in the liquor business Hannah and Hogg was formed in 1873. The label of Hannah and Hogg liquor still is available, known in the trade as bar liquor. The labels include Hannah and Hogg Rum and Hannah and Hogg Scotch. Hannah and Hogg were in partnership together, built summer residences next to each other on Mackinac Island, and were neighbors on Oak Street in Chicago. Hannah wed Catherine Grady in 1875. They had three children. They married sisters Catherine and Margaret Grady, making them brothers-in-law as well. It is now owned by George Burrows.

(Both of these beautiful summer homes feature a prominent circular tower and a wraparound porch. They also feature covered verandas, porches, towers, and balconies wrapped with diamond and fish-scale shingles. If you look closely, you will see that these two summer homes look as if they were built in reflection of each other.)

Edgecliff. Edgecliff is also known as the Wedding Cake Cottage, because it looks like a wedding cake on the outside. It was owned by William and Sarah Westover from a prominent lumbering family in Bay City, Michigan. William Westover Jr. was born in Sheffield, Massachusetts. His education was acquired at a local common school, with a touch of academy. The education he did secure and his habits served him well in future endeavors. The gold fever that swept across the country also affected William. He fared well in the gold fields. In 1852, he returned east and went to Canada and went into the lumber business. In 1853, he married Marry D. Culver of Simcoe, Ontario; she was daughter of Darius Culver of New Jersey. They had two sons, Delbert, and William Jr. In 1865, he moved to Bay City, Michigan. He beautified Bay City by erecting a business district, organized a national bank, and was presiding officer for many years. Every new railroad project was greeted genuinely, and he never turned a deserving applicant away. He built a small cottage on a national park lot in 1886, which was the first cottage built on West Bluff. Sometime in the 1890s, he picked up everything and moved to Alameda, California. He passed away in Alameda, California, on March 15, 1914.

It survived six years, changing hands twice before the Ambergs from Chicago acquired the land lease and tore it down. William Amberg was born in Bavaria and saw the cottage construction completed in 1822. He named it Inselheim, German for "Island Home," and later changed it to Edgecliff. He married Sarah Agnes Ward and had three two daughters, Mary Agnes and Genevieve, and one son, John. His occupation was in the stationary business. He founded his own company—Cameron, Amberg, and Company—only to have it destroyed by the Chicago Fire of 1871. In 1878, he started the Amberg File and Index Company and distributed his invention, the file folder. He acquired thirty patents in seven years and six hundred copyrights pertaining to the file and indexing business. Later he branched out into the quarry business, putting Amberg, Wisconsin, and Amberg Granite on the map. On Mackinac Island, his son John and Dr. McArthur established Wawashkamo Golf Club. William and John could be perfecting their game on the golf course; Amberg died after a round of golf. The cottage stayed in the family until 1942. Amberg's niece returned in 1996, reflecting on her childhood memories at Edgecliff. It is currently owned by John and Penny Barr.

(This Queen Anne is two and half stories, supports two corner towers, and is adorned with a frieze of swags across its exterior. It also has a wraparound veranda. If you look at this cottage, you will notice it has the fringe trimmed in pink. The trim is also painted in pink similar to that of a wedding cake.)

Bungalow (Hollyhock). Bungalow was built by William T. Gilbert, a relative of the Tootles, who was in the banking and lumber business in Grand Rapids, Michigan. Records show the cottage was held in the estate of William Gilbert, and his brother Thomas Gilbert and wife, Mary A. Bingham Gilbert, were the principal occupants. William and Thomas were born in Greenfield, Massachusetts. Their dad was Gen. Thomas Gilbert, who served in the army during the War of 1812. He was born on December 13, 1815. He married Harriet Arms, the daughter of Ebenezer Arms. She was a member of one of the oldest and most prominent families of the state. Mary held the title from 1904 until 1940. She brought fame to this family as a poet and daughter of a famous missionary, Abel Bingham. Reverend Abelone Bingham was a Baptist minister who was with the Baptist Missionary Union, arriving in Sault Sainte Marie in 1828. He was a very active member of the Sault Sainte Marie community, conducting a school for Indian children. One historical account lists Reverend Bingham and his daughter, a schoolteacher, as passengers aboard the first vessel to go through the Soo Locks. His mission was operated among the Ojibwa in Sault Sainte Marie, Michigan.

In Grand Rapids in 1886, she published a number of works, including a six-page Mackinac Island poem "Devil's Kitchen Mackinac Island." In an island tradition, the cottage furniture was included with the sale of the cottage. True to form, the Gilberts' dining room table continues to serve its owners and their guests with the same hospitality provided over one hundred years ago. It is currently owned by Randy and Michele Stuck from Traverse City, Michigan.

(This is a two-story carpenter Gothic frame house with scroll-sawn trim, with cross gables with a wraparound porch. In the winter of 2011–2012, the Stucks remodeled it, keeping the basic design the same but putting on different siding. The biggest change was the major landscaping project on the property.)

Cliff Cottage. Cliff Cottage was built for Chicago senator Henry Warren Leman and his wife, France E. (Dole) Leman, who were married in 1881. They had two children, Sheldon Dole and Frances M., and they enjoyed summers on Mackinac Island. Henry Leman attended law school but abandoned the practice of law to become president of the Chicago Title & Trust Company that he founded in 1890. He had served a five-year term as senator of the Sixth District of Illinois. The cottage was sold to George and Rebecca J. (Osborne) Cass of Chicago in 1893. George was nephew of the first governor of the Michigan Territory; Lewis Cass was an accomplished man of his own merit. Lewis Cass's father joined the

Continental army and fought under Gen. George Washington at Bunker Hill. Lewis Cass was born in Exeter, New Hampshire, on October 9, 1782. Lewis Cass attended Phillips Exeter Academy. The family moved to Ohio, where he became a member of the bar. In 1806, he was elected to the Ohio legislature. In 1813, Lewis Cass served as an Aide to Gen. William Henry Harrison at the Battle of Thames, a key battle in which Tecumseh was defeated and killed. In 1820, Lewis Cass led an expedition into Western Michigan, Minnesota, and Wisconsin. Cass and company found the source of the Mississippi. Lewis Cass was appointed territorial governor for the Michigan Territory by President James Madison. He was a lawyer, Supreme Court justice, ambassador, secretary of state, explorer, and territorial governor. He lived long enough to see Emancipation and died in Detroit at age eighty-four. Interment: Elmwood Cemetery in downtown Detroit. Cass's son-in-law, William Shelby, great-grandson of the first governor of Kentucky and new president of the Grand Rapids & Indiana Railroad, was next to hold title to the cottage. Shelby married Mary Kennedy Cass, George and Rebecca Cass's daughter. They held on to the title until 1908. Other notables were Louis Swift, son of Chicago pioneer meatpacker, Gustavus Franklin Swift; and the Dixon family, also of Chicago, owners of the Dixon Transfer Company. It is currently owned by the Hamady Bros. from Flint, Michigan, a supermarket chain in business from 1911 to 1991. Hamady Bros. was liquidated in 1991 after being bilked and bankrupted by the investor purchaser who received a twenty-three-year prison sentence. A Hamady store sign survived in Flint's Sloan Museum in an exhibit called Flint and the American Dream.

(It is also known as the Wonder View, and what a wonderful view it has. The name has nothing to do with Wonder Bread. It is a two-and-a-half-story Queen Anne with front-facing gable, recessed and multipaned sash windows, flared roof, along with many permutations of the rooflines and window treatments. As you come up West Bluff, it immediately catches your eye, the house and the eagle that decorates the yard.)

ANNEX

Who first settled the area known as the Annex?
Who was the person who started development in the Annex?

During the American Revolution, Ambrose Davenport, being from Virginia, was inspired to join the army. In 1796, he was able to take part in relieving the British at Fort Mackinac. He got out of the army after his enlistment was up, settled, and started a farm in what is now the Annex. The War of 1812 came to Mackinac Island. The British invaded the island. The fort surrendered to the British. The residents of the island were asked to sign their allegiance to the Crown of England. Ambrose Davenport, Samuel Abbott, and John Dousman did not. Ambrose Davenport said, "I was born in America and am determined at all hazards, to live and die an American citizen."

His wife and family were allowed to stay while he left as a prisoner. While he was away, his wife was tormented by British soldiers and residents, calling her the wife of the Yankee Rebel. Ambrose Davenport returned after the war, continued to farm, and raised a family. His cabin is still back there and is probably the oldest building on the island. He has direct descendants living all over the country today.

Gurdon Hubbard came to Mackinac Island in 1818, coming from Windsor, Vermont, as a clerk for the American Fur Company. In 1828, he bought out the company's interest in Illinois and began his career as an independent businessman. He formed the Eagle Steamship Line and a meat-packing business, organized the Chicago Board of Trade, served as a representative in the Illinois State General Assembly, and had his paws in some other businesses. His two ships were lost to maritime disasters. In 1868, his packing house was lost to fire, and in 1871, he lost the majority of his other businesses to the Great Chicago Fire. In 1855, he purchased a large portion of the eighty-acre Ambrose Davenport farm. In 1870, he built a small cottage called the Lilacs. In 1882, he got the money from some wealthy business associates to get his land surveyed and platted and divided into fourteen blocks containing 132 building lots.

The eating house was the central location for the meals. It took all the work out of preparing meals and cooking them. It was there to prevent kitchen fires. Kitchens back then were a fire hazard. All the meals were prepared and eaten in this one location. Across the street, they built the commons with a bandstand. The Annex eating house was the scene of many festive gatherings. After the eating house was closed, many of the Annex cottagers sometimes joined other cottagers in preparing meals or eating in one of the island hotels. They outfitted their kitchens with stoves and cupboards filled with pots, pans, silverware, and fine china. In contrast to East and West Bluff where the land was owned by the state park and the house was privately owned, in the Annex, the house and the land were both privately owned.

As we enter the Annex, the first house that you notice is the Hospitality Cottage. What you will notice as you drive or walk back there is that it is very spacious. This was built in 1885 by Hugh and Emma McCurdy. McCurdy was asked to dedicate the guest register at the grand opening of the Grand Hotel on July 10, 1887. It is owned by R. D. Musser III, the current president of the Grand Hotel. The Pink House is the children's playhouse.

(Widows are the center of this clapboard Queen Anne summerhouse with a sweeping, curved veranda. The front gable features matching roundels flanking paired centered double-hung casement windows. Centered in the front gable is a Palladian window. Yet another oval window fills the span between the gable and the three-story turret. Barred half-circle ventilation openings line the base of the porch, while multipaned windows complete the interesting appearance of this cottage.)

The Lake Cliff Cottage was built by Francis and Betsy Stockbridge in 1884. Stockbridge was one of the successful lumber barons of the era. He was born in Bath, Maine, in 1826. He entered the business world at sixteen, leaving home to clerk in a dry-goods store in Boston. He moved to Chicago, where he opened a lumberyard, amassing a great fortune. He moved to Saugatuck where he could be closer to the trees. While in Saugatuck, he built a number of sawmills. The mills turned out millions of board feet of lumber. He married a local girl, Elizabeth Foster Arnold, better known as Betsy. They had one child; it was a son named Joseph. Betsy was somewhat eccentric, dignified, and austere. She was loved by all who knew her. At this time, his political career took off, serving in the Michigan legislature from 1869 to 1873. At this time, lumbering operations were moving north. Stockbridge and Johnson relocated their lumbering operations to Saint Ignace, in the Upper Peninsula, closer to the trees. They formed both the Mackinac Lumber Co. and the Black River Lumber Co. Stockbridge was president of both. Stockbridge lived in Kalamazoo.

Francis Stockbridge, along with his brother-in-law, George Arnold, from Allegan County, became involved with Mackinac Island. George started the Arnold Line Ferry Company in 1889 and built the Brigadoon. He bought land on the southwest side of the island with a commanding view of the Straits of Mackinac. This was the site where the Grand Hotel would be built. Like the Grand Hotel, the Lake Cliff has the same commanding view of the Straits of Mackinac. Stockbridge was smart enough to know that he wanted a hotel but did not want to have anything to with the building or running of a hotel. He sold his land contingent upon the hotel suiting him. Stockbridge was openhearted, whole-souled, and generous. As a politician, he was distinguished not only as a keen businessman but also as a skilled organizer and as a calm, insightful, and prudent manager. After being elected to the US Senate and spending most of their time moving around in those circles in Washington, DC, they came to the realization that they had little time for Mackinac Island. Stockbridge and his family, after entering the political arena, had little time for Mackinac Island. He sold the cottage in late 1889 to Michael Cudahy. Betsy's brother George and family were full-time residents, and nephew George Stockbridge had a West Bluff cottage. Both could provide the Stockbridges accommodations when they were on the island. Michael Cudahy purchased the cottage from Mr. Stockbridge. The sale included the furnishings, and for the $7,000 purchase price, Stockbridge agreed to build a dock and a footpath down the bluff. Michael Cudahy sold this cottage to his brother Edward in 1887, developed land in California for several years, moved back to Mackinac Island, and built the Inn at Stone Cliff. The cottage is now owned by Dr. Disiaba and his family from Manchester, Indiana. It was bought by Dr. Disiaba in 1966.

The story goes something like this: Whomever Dr. Disiaba bought the cottage from was interested in having it owned by a family. There were interested parties who were interested in using it as a retreat for the corporation for its business partners; the sellers were not having any of it. They wanted it to be owned by a family.

(The Cudahys remodeled the original Stockbridge cottage into a Queen Anne. It is not certain which owner built the four-story round tower with a conical roof. It has an open-air fourth floor. The view is something to desire.)

The Lilacs was built by the Hubbards in 1870 when he was sixty-eight. Perhaps to escape the sweltering heat and the problems he was going through, he had the Lilacs built. After everything was done, all that the Hubbards had left was the land on Mackinac Island and the cottage, the Lilacs.

(This carpenter Gothic–design cottage has had some additions since the original owners. The window in the front gable became a door, and the front door became three windows. The porch was expanded to accommodate the rearranged entry. The remodeling followed the Caskey tradition of cottage design but lacked carpenter Gothic ornamentation.)

The Meta Mura. Dr. Linn McArthur had a hand in this cottage, because one of his patients, the Puttkammers. The situation was this: They were advised by Dr. McArthur to get their son out of the city heat and up to Mackinac in the summer for the sake of the child's health. They rented the Lilacs for three summers, bought land, and watched the construction of their home until completion.

(The original was a small two-bedroom one-story bungalow. As years passed, they added a second floor, porches, sunrooms, and importantly, bathrooms. It has a style of its own, little in common with the Caskey cottages that are around it, except the cross gable. Latin for *walls* was used to convey the meaning "Meta's House," with the musical name Meta Mura, literally translated "Walls of Meta.")

The cottage across the street is also owned by the Puttkammers, and it is a year-round residence. The Puttkammer cottage is probably the only one that is still owned by an original family member. A Puttkammer built it back in the 1800s, and a Puttkammer still owns it today. The Annex includes quaint carpenter Gothic and colonial revival cottages.

THE GOVERNOR'S SUMMER RESIDENCE

How many governors have spent time at the residence?

What happens if the state no longer wants to use the residence?

Lawrence and Mabel Young had been married eight years before moving into their new Mackinac Island home. Lawrence Young was born in Louisville, Kentucky. His father, Colonel Bennett H. Young, was a distinguished Confederate officer and a noted lawyer. While at Princeton University, Lawrence Young pitched on the baseball team for four years and was the captain of the team his senior year. He graduated in 1892 and enrolled in law school at the University of Louisville, close to his father's law practice.

Louisville, Kentucky, is well-known for its horses and horse racing. Perhaps through their mutual interest in horses, Lawrence Young met and married Mabel Wheeler in 1894. Her father, George Henry Wheeler, was president of the Washington Park Club, the best known race track in America. Lawrence Young later served multiple terms as president and also chaired the Western Jockey Club for five years. The Western Jockey Club controlled all racing in the West and South, setting racing dates and disciplining all jockeys and horse owners. Wheeler was president of the Chicago Railway Company. Lawrence Young joined his father-in-law in the company, serving as vice president and then as director upon Wheeler's death. Lawrence Young continued to practice law and was appointed assistant corporation counsel for the city of Chicago for a term.

Lawrence Young hired a fellow member of the Washington Park Club and the Saddle and Cycle Club architect Fredrick W. Perkins to design a residence for the beautiful west fort lot that he and Mable had leased from the Mackinac Island State Park Commission. Local contractor Patrick Doud supervised a large crew of seventy-five craftsmen to execute Perkins's design over the winter of 1901–1902. He contracted to complete the project for $15,000; however, Mable paid Doud $500 bonus to express her delight with her new summer residence.

Mabel died in her early forties on July 15, 1915, at the cottage that so delighted her. Eight years later, Lawrence Young married Mrs. Sarah Caldwell Smith. One year later, at the age of fifty-four, he died. Clara and Hugo Scherer bought the cottage in 1926. They sold it in 1945 to the Mackinac Island State Park Commission for use as the Michigan governor's summer residence. The park paid the Scherer family $15,000, the same price the Youngs paid for it.

This place has probably cut more deals for the state of Michigan than the state house down in Lansing. Due to the relationship between Mackinac Island State Park and the National Park Service, if the state of Michigan desires to no longer own the governor's summer residence, the property will revert back to the National Park's control.

31/01/2005

Some Facts

The house was built in the winter of 1901–1902 by Chicago attorney Lawrence A. Young at a cost of $15,000. The architect was Frederick W. Perkins (1866–1928), also of Chicago.

The builder was local contractor Patrick Doud, great-uncle of the current mayor of the city of Mackinac Island, Margaret Doud. Doud employed seventy-five islanders who took three months to build the house.

The interior is Georgia yellow pine, and the exterior is Michigan white pine. The exterior shingles were originally stained dark green, with deep-red trim. The roof is made of cedar shingles.

The house is approximately 7,100 square feet and has three stories, eleven bedrooms, nine-and-a-half bathrooms, and a basement. In 1944, the house was purchased by the Mackinac Island State park Commission from the Hugo and Clara Scherer family. The commission paid $15,000, the original construction cost.

Prisoners were brought to the island to renovate the home in time for the thirty-seventh annual governor's conference in July 1 to 4, 1945, under the supervision of First Lady Anne Kelly.

Senator John F. Kennedy and Governor G. Mennen Williams met in the sun porch on June 2, 1960, when Kennedy was seeking William's endorsement to be president.

President Bill Clinton visited while he was governor of Arkansas. Other presidents to visit were George H. W. Bush, Gerald Ford, and Harry Truman.

Ten governors have used the summer residence (Harry F. Kelly, Kim Sigler, G. Mennen Williams, John B. Swainson, George Romney, William G. Milliken, James J. Blanchard, John M. Engler, Jennifer Granholm, and Rick Snyder.)

The house was painted white in 1945 for the governor's conference.

An elevator was added in 1961 for Governor Swainson.

First Lady Helen Milliken designed the garden beds in the 1970s.

An exterior staircase as a fire escape was added in 1977 for Gerald Ford's visit.

The last renovation of the residence took place during the Engler Administration in 1996–1997.

All renovations were done through private funds.

The gazebo from *Somewhere in Time* used to reside at the governor's summer residence. Around the spring of 2010, it was renovated and moved to its current location east of Fort Mackinac near Anne's Tablet. The gazebo can now be rented for weddings.

(It is reminiscent of the transitional shingle style, fading by 1901, but with hints of the evolving arts and crafts style. This is evident in the large hipped roof with dramatic flaring eves. Gabled dormers with similar flaring eves project from the roofline. The walls and roof are finished with wood shingles, once painted a dark color to blend with nature. The foundation walls and chimneys are native limestone. Immediately west of Fort Mackinac and 125 feet above Lake Huron, the dormer windows and wide verandas provide a sweeping view of the Straits of Mackinac.)

Anne's Tablet

Who is Anne?

I was having some problems in my life during my first few years as an employee here on Mackinac Island and was looking for a quiet place to sort things out. An acquaintance mentioned to me Anne's Tablet. The spot is about one acre in size and overlooks the harbor and also Anne's Cottage. This place is located on the island's East Bluff. This place is dedicated to author Constance Fenimore Woolson; she is great-niece to James Fenimore Cooper, author of *Last of the Mohicans*. From 1850 to about 1895, she spent a great deal of time here on Mackinac Island. When she was here, she spent it at what is now Anne's Cottage. It was also the setting in the book. In 1882, she wrote the book *Anne* about a little girl who grew up here on Mackinac Island during the Victorian Era. You will find this a very beautiful, restful, and quiet place to go for reflection. What makes it so special for me is the price that has to be paid to get there. One has to walk up a ton of steps and then walk up a hill to get there. There is no spot on the island as dear to me as Anne's Tablet is. This is where I first learned my tour. I had a problem reciting someone else's information; I had to make it my own. It is also a place that I like to go to when I have a lot of weight on my shoulders. I will go up there and reflect on the problem, sometimes coming up with a solution, more often just feeling better and the weight off my shoulders.

East Bluff

Crow's Nest. Valcoln Warsaw Mather was born on May 5, 1847. Dr. Valcoln and Olive were married on July 24, 1871, in Huntington, Cabell County, West Virginia. In 1900, Dr. Valcoln Warsaw Mather, with his wife, Olive S. (Keith) Mather, and their two children, Leila and Henry, left the heat of Kansas City, Missouri, and came to spend the summer on Mackinac Island. Mather's medical career began in Kansas City, under the tutelage of Dr. V. R. Moss and later Dr. Joseph Field. Mather completed his training at Pulte Medical College in Cincinnati, Ohio, in 1873, and practiced briefly in West Virginia. Henry joined his father's medical practice and became a surgeon of some note. Henry and Leila were both young adults when their parents built the Mackinac Island cottage.

Off to the west in the woods, a trail leads to Anne's Tablet. This memorial honors Constance Fenimore Woolson, author of *Anne*, a popular 1880s novel about a young girl's adventures on Mackinac Island during the fur trade era. In admiration of their Aunt Constance, the Samuel Mather family from Cleveland erected Anne's Tablet in 1916. What is interesting is that Samuel Mather and Valcoln Mather shared a common ancestor, Timothy Mather. Timothy's brother was Rev. Cotton Mather, known in history for his participation in the Salem Witch Trials. (It is currently owned by Dr. Ledtke.)

(The Crow's Nest is the last cottage to be built on the East Bluff. Local carpenter Frank Rounds constructed this small colonial revival cottage so that nothing obscured the view from the enclosed front porch. At the same time, its six-pane glass windows and the sidelights flanking the front door and the transom above shelter the residents from the breezes of the Straits of Mackinac.)

The Cliffs. Local contractor Mathias Elliot built this cottage, the Cliffs, in 1890. The first owner, Mr. Henry Freeman, worked for the First National Bank in Fort Wayne, Indiana. In 1941, the cottage was bought by Little Stone Church. First owner, Mr. Henry Freeman, worked as a cashier at First National Bank in Fort Wayne, Indiana. He also was associated in business with other East Bluff cottagers from Fort Wayne, Indiana: Hamilton, Bursley, Taylor, and Bond. In 1941, the Congregational Church, or the Little Stone Church as it is known on the island, acquired the cottage. Twenty years later, the family of former Governor Frank D. Fitzgerald, former Michigan Supreme Court Justice John Fitzgerald, and Michigan State Representative Frank Fitzgerald owned the cottage from 1961 until the present.

(Simple ornamentation makes this gabled cottage elegant and unified, typical of carpenter Gothic. The intersecting gable gives a symmetrical look to the Cliffs. The second-floor window and the balustrade balcony line up over the extra-wide central stairway that rises to the ample first-floor porch. Current owners are the Bedours.)

Fisher Cottage. The original owner was Elstner Fisher from Cincinnati, Ohio. He was forty years old when he had this cottage built. His career with the United States Navy and his job with the Pennsylvania Railroad companies made him a traveling man. With the navy, he was assigned duty on the steamer *Vandalia* and sailed on a Mediterranean cruise during the Turko-Russian War in 1879. In 1879, as assistant navigator, he sailed on the steamer *Wachusett* in the North Atlantic. Later, he sailed through the Straits of Magellan to Lima, Peru, where the ship officials negotiated the Chile-Peru peace talks. Stateside, Fisher's next assignment found him surveying the shoreline of the Eastern Seaboard from Connecticut to South Carolina. He resigned from the navy in 1884 and started a new career with the Pennsylvania Railroad. In 1887, he accepted the position of assistant engineer for the Michigan Central Railroad.

The Michigan Central Railroad kept him moving with its changing districts and divisions. As a trainmaster, Mr. Fisher's job required keeping the trains on schedule, as published in the timetables. He moved from Jackson, Michigan, to Detroit, where he helped the city survey for a tunnel under the Detroit River. His promotion to assistant superintendent took him to Hamilton, Ontario, to become general superintendent and chief engineer of the Toronto, Hamilton, & Buffalo railroad line. This career apparently kept him in one place long enough to marry Sarah Burt of Detroit.

(Carpenter G. W. Catell built a Dutch colonial on this lot in 1893, but an extensive renovation left little to the original structure. The historical architecture was still represented through its prominent three-stage corner tower topped with a bell roof. This was previously owned by Michigan's US senator Phillip Hart and his wife, Jane (Briggs) Hart, in the 1950s.

Phil Hart was wounded in the Normandy invasion on June 6, 1944, D-day. Phil Hart became the conscience of the senate. Senator Hart was the former lieutenant governor of Michigan from 1954 to 1959, serving under Governor G. Mennen Williams, Paul and Maryanke Alexander, living in Mount Pleasant, Michigan, with three dogs, four cats, and six horses. He has five children, and they have been summer residents of Mackinac Island for the past six years.)

The Tootle. The Tootle is one of the most distinctive cottages on the island. This was built in 1888 by Patrick Doud. This was designed in the same style as the Tootle mansion in Saint Joseph, Missouri. It was originally owned by Milton Jr. and Lillian (Duckworth) Tootle. The family fortune came from Milton Sr. and Catherine (O'Neill) Tootle, whose merchandise outlet outfitted gold panners and pioneer settlers of the western frontier. Milton Tootle Sr. even founded a town of his own, Miltonvale, Kansas, where the Tootle Fest is held every year in August. It remained in the Tootle family for fifty years. It is currently owned by the Timmons family from Missoula, Montana.

(It is a two-story iconic-order porch with railings and leaded glass windows. What really help make this cottage stand out are the gardens. Many of the plants and trees from Tootle's landscaping efforts do survive and flourish on this lot and also on neighboring lots. The unusual one-hundred-year-old trees on the front lawn are Camperdown elm, a grafted tree also known as umbrella elm or weeping elm. This variety of tree originated from a seedling at Camperdown House, near Dundee, Scotland, and is a cultivar of the Scotch elm. The leaves show a high degree of asymmetry at the base and are dark green in color. The drooping branches have made it attractive as a small-scale landscaping tree.)

The Dolce and Domum. It is also known now as the Myron and Maynard. It is distinguished as the first cottage built on land leased in the National Park. It still remains the simple carpenter Gothic built by Charles Caskey over a hundred years ago.

Warren Cottage. Warren Cottage is affectionately known as the Baby Grand. If you look at it closely, it does resemble a baby grand piano. John Esaias Warren was a diplomat, lawyer, travel writer, real estate investor, and mayor of Saint Paul, Minnesota. He married Charlotte Warren. Their two children, Mary N. "Nina" and Paul, were born in Minnesota. His writing produced *Tropics of Times*, *Para; or Scenes and Adventures on the Banks of the Amazon*, and *Vagamundo, or the Attaché in Spain*. He took up residence in Brussels, Belgium, a year after building their small carpenter Gothic cottage. He died in Brussels in 1886. The cottage sold the year before to Charles C. Bowen of Detroit. Charles Bowen converted the simple Caskey-designed cottage into an elaborate double house connected by a giant iconic portico. Two dramatic semicircular projections run the entire breadth of the two separate houses, with a T-shaped house on the west, probably the original cottage. Another gabled structure on the east was connected to form one stately beaux arts classical dwelling. There is a story for this cottage. It was owned by two brothers, and it was two separate houses; the carriageway was in the middle. When the carriage stopped, each brother would depart the carriage and go to their proper homes. Where the front door is now is where the carriageway was. It is now owned by Dr. Louis Putz, a radiologist down in Bloomfield Hills, Michigan. His wife, Marilyn, plays piano sometimes down at Mission Point Resort and at Sainte Anne's Catholic Church.

Morrison Cottage. When Anne Morrison had the cottage built in 1891, she was the oldest of three children born to Mary and Robert Morrison of Delaware, Ohio, and had never married. The Morrisons kept the cottage on Mackinac Island until 1900. When the Morrisons sold the cottage to Fannie Owen Lathrop, she was also the widow of George Howard Lathrop and daughter of Jane and John Owen. The families who summered here on Mackinac Island found opportunities to share their discovery of Mackinac with their relatives and friends. Phoebe Hamilton acquired the lease in the mid-1920s. It was also owned by Bill Terwilliger, who should've been in the Olympics in 1942 as he was national decathlon champion but missed out because of the war; there was no Olympics until 1948. He was in the trials against Bob Mathias, and he came in fourth, and they took the top three. So no Olympics. It is now owned by Tom and Sandy Phillips from Bellevue, Washington.

CEMETERIES

Where were the Catholic and Protestant cemeteries located?
How many unmarked graves are at the Post Cemeteries?
How many total graves at the Post Cemetery?
Why are the civilians in the Post Cemetery?

In 1779, the settlement moved their log Catholic Church to the island from Fort Michilimackinac, across ice to the south shore of Mackinac Island. The church was located in the area of what is now the Village Inn. The cemetery was located across the street from the church. Both cemeteries were located in town. It was originally established for the use of Roman Catholics; other Mackinac Islanders eventually used this cemetery. The borough of Mackinac Island closed both Roman Catholic and Protestant graveyards in the 1850s. The Roman Catholic cemetery was filled to capacity, and the growing village prevented expansion into adjoining lots. In 1856, the Protestant cemetery, long since abandoned by the mission, was declared a public nuisance. The islanders chose the tranquil forest along Garrison Road for their new cemeteries.

Sainte Anne's. Sainte Anne's was previously located on the corner of Hoban Street and Market Street. In 1924, the island disinterred most of the graves and moved them to the central part of the island. The green and gold marker in the center of the cemetery is that of Mary Biddle, the daughter of Edward and Agatha Biddle down on Market Street. She died of unknown causes in 1833. That is the oldest known grave there at Sainte Anne's. Phil Hart is buried here. He was a WWII veteran, lieutenant governor, and US senator. He was also co-sponsor of the 1964 Civil Rights Act. Also buried here are some of the families that helped settle the island and also run the island today.

Protestant cemetery. The Protestant cemetery is referred to as the Mackinac Island Cemetery. Buried here is G. Mennen Williams, governor of Michigan from 1949 to 1961. He was also known as Soapy Williams and later on served as chief justice of the state Supreme Court and as a federal official in the Departments of State and Justice. He was also the soap fortune heir to Mennen Soap Products, which was the family business. The green and gold marker is that of Herriot Mitchell. She died of unknown causes in 1830. It is the oldest known grave there at the Protestant cemetery. Buried here are the people that helped settle the island and still live here today.

Post Cemetery. Buried here are active-duty personnel who served at Fort Mackinac, dependents of active-duty personnel, and civilians. This practice of burying civilians dates back to 1804. Mackinac Island State Park and the Veterans Administration are charged with the upkeep of the Post Cemetery. There are about 108 graves all together, and sixty-nine are known but to God. Phil Porter, in his State Park Pamphlet Mackinac Island's Post Cemetery, blamed post commanders of the past for a number of the unknowns. They kept poor records and did not maintain the site. Some of the unknowns have since been identified.

Until 2010, there were three unmarked graves. One of the unmarked was gravesite K-8, which was thought to be that of Sarah Walsh, who was thought to be the stillborn death of the Walsh family. Through records search and research, descendants of the Walsh family identified the infant as being Robert D. Walsh. On November 17, 2010, at 10:00 a.m. at the Post Cemetery, State Park Director Phil Porter and Park Operations Robert McGreevy placed a headstone at the gravesite. Post Cemetery flag continually flies at half-staff. This cemetery is one of four national cemeteries with this honor. The others are the National Memorial Cemetery of the Pacific (the Punchbowl) in Honolulu, Hawaii; Arlington National Cemetery in Arlington, Virginia; and the National Cemetery at Gettysburg in Gettysburg, Pennsylvania.

GEOLOGICAL FEATURES

What type of rock is Mackinac Island primarily made of?

What were the processes that formed most of the geological features of Mackinac Island?

What type of rock is limestone?

"What a beautiful and thrilling specimen for America to preserve and hold up to the view of her refined citizens and the world, in future ages! It is a Nation's Park; containing man, and beast, in all the wild and freshness of their nature's beauty!" These geological features that I am about to talk about are probably the very reason why Mackinac Island became our nation's second national park. Mackinac Island is a huge chunk of limestone in the middle of Lake Huron. The features that I am about to talk about are Robinson's Folly, Arch Rock, Devil's Kitchen, Lovers Leap, Crack in the Island, Cave of the Woods, Sugar Loaf, and Skull Cave.

Mackinac Island is made up primarily of Mackinac breccia and limestone as being the prominent rock types. The hardened Mackinac breccia is pretty easy to recognize in a formation by its pockmarked surface that is caused by weathering of breccia fragments. The more soluble fragments are removed, leaving large cavities in the formation, giving rise to well-developed pockmarked surface. Erosion of the regional limestone by the glacial lakes has removed the less-hardened material enclosing the hardened breccia masses. Mackinac Island has been affected by recent glaciation of the Wisconsin period and glacial Lakes Algonquin and Nipissing, following retreat of the glaciers. Glacial Lake Algonquin represents an age of eleven thousand to twelve thousand years, and glacial Lake Nipissing represents an age of approximately four thousand years.

Robinson's Folly

After the removal of the fort to the island in 1780, Captain Robinson, who then commanded the post, had a summerhouse built upon this cliff. This soon became a place of frequent resort for himself and his brother officers. Pipes, cigars, and wine were called into requisition, for at that time, no hospitality or entertainment was complete without them, and thus many an hour that would have been lonely and tedious passed pleasantly away. After a few years, however, by the action of the elements, a portion of this cliff, with the summerhouse, was precipitated to the base of the rocks, which disastrous event gave rise to the name. Around the beach below is a confused mass of debris, the remains, doubtless, of the fall.

Robinson's Folly is 127 feet above present level of Lake Huron. It represents a prominent portion of the sea cliffs formed along the eastern side of Mackinac Island through the erosive action of Lake Nipissing.

Arch Rock

This rock formation was looked upon with awe by the Indian as the bridge over which departed souls could find their last resting place in the island caves.

Along the beaches of Lake Huron, there was a band of Chippewa (Ojibwa). There, lodges were round topped and built from saplings and elm bark. In the finest lodge lived the chief; his lodge was the finest. The door consisted of moose hide. The chief had a beautiful daughter named She-who-walks-like-the-mist. She worked hard and never complained about it. Her father was proud and knew that someday she would marry and have many sons. For a while, She-who-walks-like-the-mist was smiling and offering wild rice to the young men who were coming to the lodge bearing. Suddenly she was with downcast eyes and not welcoming anymore. Her father became very angry.

"Two moons ago, as I paddled to the eastern shore of our village, a handsome brave appeared to me. His clothes were of the whitest deerskin covered with designs my fingers have never made and my eyes have never seen. But even more wonderful was his robe of light. He spoke. 'Oh lovely one,' he said. 'Long have I watched you in the village, wishing that you might be mine for all time. In my home high above you I am the son of a chief, Evening Star, and I am therefore a Sky Person. My father gave me permission to descend to earth that I might ask you to join me in my sky home.'"

"And what was your answer, my daughter?"

"I said I would marry no one but him," Mist woman answered.

"No! It is forbidden. You shall marry no one at all!" Seizing her by the arms, placing her in the bow of his war canoe, with mighty strokes he drove the craft to the Island of Turtle Spirits. He drew his cord made of deer sinew and threw the noose about Mist Woman, dragging her toward the rock that towered above the beach. After securely tying her, "Now," said he, "you shall not see your lover again. Here shall you lie until you decide to be a faithful daughter once more." Off he went.

Mist Woman did not cry out. Tears flowed down upon the rock, speaking of her longing. Little by little the tears melted the stone until an arch appeared, and she left on a high bridge. That night, through the arch appeared the rays of the evening star, and here came her star brave. Gathering her in his arms, off they went into the land of the Sky People. The tears that could not melt the heavy heart of a father melted the stone on Mackinac Island.

Arch Rock is one of the most striking features of the island and one of the reasons why the island became a national park. It is also the best-known and most striking rock formation on the island. Arch Rock was more than likely the byproduct of wave action undermining and removing the softer material and leaving the firmer breccia as a natural bridge. The bridge is approximately 146 feet above Lake Huron. It has a span of forty to fifty feet and is ten feet thick. Breccia is a rock composed of broken fragments of minerals or rocks cemented together by fine grained matrix that can be either similar to or different from the composition of the fragments. People do marriage proposals, spelling out in the water below Will You Marry Me. It is also one of two natural arch rock formations east of the Mississippi; the other is Arches Natural Bridge near Lexington, Virginia.

Sunset Rock

A.k.a. Chimney Rock, it was created by selective removal and erosion of less-resistant limestone enveloping the more hardened breccia forming the vertical column of rock, making up Chimney Rock by glacial Lake Nipissing. The breccia column remains attached to the headlands, so Chimney Rock is not a sea stack. Sea stacks are isolated by themselves, and chimney stacks are still attached to the headlands.

Devil's Kitchen

Near the cave of the Red Gee-bis were Wen-di-goes, or cannibal giants. A little girl and her grandfather stayed behind on Mackinac Island as the rest of the tribe departed for the winter. Her grandfather was old and blind. The tribe had deserted him, and the granddaughter, who was young and beautiful, was staying behind to care for him. Grand daughter's was named Willow Wand. Grandfather did not want his granddaughter to stay with him. "You are young and beautiful, and you should have gone with our people, for it is there that your young man, Kee-we-naw, will seek you."

"He will find me, Grandfather, though I was hidden in the deepest cave."

Blind and helpless, he knew the dangers that surrounded them; he could only hope that Git-chi-Man-i-tou would protect them. Willow Wand placed a white deerskin with vermillion high on the cliff so the fishermen will see it and come to their rescue. Enemies might also see it. They would kill Grandfather; granddaughter would serve out her years as a slave. Enemy warriors were unlikely to come to this spot, for they too feared the red devils. Staying out of sight of Devil's Kitchen, Willow Wand readied a cave that she and Grandfather found. While readying the evening meal, Willow Wand saw some movement far back in the cave. Seizing a blazing stick from the fire, she stood with a hard-beating heart as a huge black shape moved toward her. It was Mag-wah, the she-bear. Slowly she backed out to the ledge.

"What is it, child?" asked the grandfather.

"Yaw! It is Mag-wah! If I am quick, perhaps I can kill her with my bows and arrows."

"Let us all live in peace. Let her sleep in her lodge that we may sleep in ours."

She-bear turned on her flat paws and disappeared back into the cave. Together the girl and her grandfather lay down to sleep after eating their scanty meal. As night came, the sun sank and coolness came, telling the old one of the coming night. With it, he knew there would come the cries of the tortured ones waiting to be roasted above the cooking fires. The grandfather did not fear death; he lived too long among wild beasts and painted warriors. He worried that he could not warn his granddaughter of danger.

Granddaughter was whimpering in her sleep, pleading for water. Mother of Willow Wand, who was on her deathbed, had whispered this secret to him. The girl had inherited a magic gift from her father, a gift that, used rightly, would give her the powers of a medicine woman. She unknowingly had the power to bring springs of pure water from the earth in any quantity she desired. She could not be told of this power until she had undergone seven days of fasting to become a woman. Then she could be told.

Each night she went to sleep crying out for water, and each night the cry for water got a little louder. Painfully the grandfather made his way into the cave where Willow Wand was crying loudly in her sleep for water. As Grandfather got near, Willow Wand opened her eyes. Leaping to her feet, she struck the rock with her hand and cried, "Water!" Instantly, a tiny stream burst out from the rocks. Willow Wand gave a loud scream, and together they both drank from it. Grandfather told the story of her gift and how it should be used for good and never in jest. Grandfather finally drifted off to sleep, gently covering him with a robe. She knelt near the edge of the cliff to watch.

From the cave of the Red Gee-bis, she saw the red glare of cooking fires followed by terrible shrieks of the captives. Awakened by the sounds, Mag-wah, the she-bear, came out from her cave to stand close to the girl. She felt no fear, thinking this was no regular bear but one bewitched by an evil magician into the bear shape. Across the round top islands, a storm arose, tossing black clouds across the sky. Birds of evil shape sailed overhead, and all living things on the island fled for shelter. It was even louder than the wind raising the screams of the victims below. To Willow Wand's horror, she saw the figure of a young man being dragged, bound, into the evil cave. It was Kee-we-naw, her beloved.

It was then that the Red-Gee-bis looked up and saw Willow Wand kneeling on the ledge. He held up his hand to stop the ceremonies, for he recognized her as the holder of the wand of power, and this he desired. In threatening tones, he demanded the hand of Willow Wand. She laughed at him and ordered him gone. He leaped off the cliff above, intending to drop down and carry off the girl. As he sprang, she struck the wall with a mighty blow, sending out such a gush of water that it not only flung the devil straight to the bottom of the Demon's Hole but also quenched the fires of the Gee-bis. O-kies and the devils were trying in vain to rekindle their cooking fires. Willow Wand sent a rainbow mist to serve as a bridge, and in the next moment, Kee-we-naw was at her side.

It was now dawn, and her task was not yet complete. Escaping demons that were drowned in the lake, she put out the fires forever, and by nightfall, the cave of horrors was empty. Kee-we-naw told them how he found their tribe to the south. And he was directed to the Island. It was there that he saw the vermillion-painted deerskin. When he started toward the beach, a pair of beautifully decorated moccasins had floated by. He put them on his feet and was transported to the Devil's Cave.

The following spring, when the people returned, they found Willow Wand and her husband and Grandfather living comfortably in the cave. They kept warm all winter on the firewood left by the Red Gee-bis. This was the end of the terrors of the Wen-di-goes, where they once roasted and ate men, the Devil's Kitchen.

Devil's Kitchen is a product of the recent interaction of the shoreline of Mackinac Island and the waters of Lake Huron. Earlier erosion by glacial Lake Nipissing may also have had some influence. Although shallow, Devil's Kitchen is visited a lot because of its location on Mackinac Island, on M-185, the state highway that circles the Island. A local legend alleges that the Native Americans of the Straits of Mackinac considered the cave to be ominous, a location inhabited by bad spirits. Allegedly, the spirits were cannibals who would capture and eat victims who ventured too close to the ill-omened location. The cave is blackened with soot to this day, allegedly from the evil spirits' cooking fires, hence the name Devil's Kitchen.

Sugar Loaf

Man-a-boz-ho was, to the Indian, a person of miraculous birth who served as a messenger of the Great Spirit. He was believed capable of superhuman feats yet, at the same time, was a man with man's weaknesses and foolishness, which brought him much closer to the Indians themselves. First, he was brought up as a child and learned man's customs, built a lodge, hunted and fished, sang his war songs and medicine songs, and went to war. He suffered defeat and victory. Sometimes he wandered half starving. Because he lived the lives of the people, his magic powers were never beyond the belief of the people themselves.

Many moons to the south, there were those who wished he stayed among them. Ten of these were young men who, as children, had listened to the storytellers weaving their magic with tales of the brave and the foolish deeds of the mighty Man-a-boz-ho. Now as young men, the ten wished to find this great magician so that he might grant each the special wish they held deep in their hearts. They banded together, determined to seek him out. For five moons, they traveled over places where other moccasins had not trod, places haunted only by spirits.

At last they came to the broad water where far on the horizon lay an island shaped like a sleeping turtle. Summoning up their courage, they at last drove their canoes into the beach and started in single file toward the rocks and forest above them. It was there they found him, an old man whose long hair bore the mark of winter snow, seated in front of his lodge. One who served as leader moved forward and placed his gifts of tobacco and wampum on the deer hide upon which the old Man-i-tou rested.

"We have come, O-me-shaw-me-see-maw, Grandfather, to ask a final boon that we may be men among men. Will you grant our wishes?"

Man-a-boz-ho bent his head, nodding, so that his eagle plumes tossed in the lake breeze. "Ne-ga-wob, I shall see," he answered, and his voice was like Ke-nu, the thunderbird, at a great distance.

The first youth then asked that he be turned into a great war chief that he might drive the enemies to the east and west from the lands of his people. His wish was granted. The second wished to be a great hunter. The wish was granted. The third asked to be a great and powerful shaman or medicine man. Again the wish was granted. The fourth asked to be a strong dancer, the fifth asked to be an orator, speaking wise words for all to listen; the sixth, a teller of legends; the seventh, a maker of swift canoes; the eighth, the handsomest of braves; the ninth, the fastest runner and the strongest in games. And Man-a-boz-ho granted them all their wishes.

The tenth stepped forward and placed his gifts "I wish that I may never die but that I shall live for all time."

Man-a-boz-ho was angered. "You have asked the one gift no mortal can have, eternal life. But because I have given my word that all gifts will be granted, eternal life is yours."

While the others watched, they saw their friend grow, twist, change shape, until he became a tall rock. There he stands today, unmoving, in the sun, snow, and storm, viewing the lake with eyes that cannot see. He that had been given eternal life was without life forever.

Your word should be golden, and be careful what you wish for.

Sugar Loaf is the largest of several stacks on the island. It is a Lake Algonquin shoreline feature. The most plausible theory for the formation of the breccia is that salt beds deposited during the Silurian period were dissolved, forming vast caverns into which the overlying Silurian and Devonian limestone beds collapsed and were recemented. Sugar Loaf stands about three hundred feet from the Ancient Island (a.k.a. Fort Holmes). Sugar Loaf is approximately seventy-nine feet high using the road as the base. Sugar Loaf is a sea stack that is the product of Lake Algonquin. It is a sea stack because it is isolated by itself. There is a stairway that will take you up to Point Lookout, where you can get a wonderful aerial view not only of Sugar Loaf but of the area as well.

Skull Cave

The great chief, Ke-nu, the thunderbird, was troubled. Long ago, he was the maker of peace pipes, molding them between his fingers from the red clay. During that time, there was peace in the tribe. Now that he had become chief for many years, there was endless bickering, which grew louder and tiresome each day. It was time to consult Mich-i-bou the Great Hare for the answer.

After speaking with the prophets and after fasting, he was ready. He first went to Red Clay Hill. Here, as of old, he took a great mound of pipe clay and went toward the Place of Skulls. There, in this sacred place, far from human haunts, he knew that Mich-i-bou would be waiting.

Ke-nu knew he must find the way of peace, for his heart was heavy. He, the thunderbird, had been a great warrior, but he had not become so by fighting with mere women. And yet the sound of their wrangling had grown so loud that he now eagerly sought the quiet of Skull Cave even though it contained rows of skulls and skeletons of dead warriors. Even the spirits of air and of earth had lacked the power to frighten the women in silence. Only Mich-i-bou could help him by turning the soft clay into true peace pipes so that the smoker might once more know true brotherhood.

While in the cave, waiting for the voice of Mich-i-bou, he traced designs in the sand of the pipe bowls, which he would make if the Great Hare gave his permission. Suddenly, a skeleton rolled toward him from the cave basin. Ke-nu drew back, afraid. But the skeleton spoke, saying, "Do not fear me. Under thy feet you will find soft copper. Out of it I shall make tubes a pipe's length and in their sides pierce a small hole for a peace note. You may then place therein a reed that makes a sweet sound. Then shall you cover them with clay and place them to dry. Next, with thumb and forefinger fashion, the pipe bowls you have drawn." And the clacking sound of the skull grew silent.

Ke-nu eagerly set to work. As spoken, he found soft copper beneath his feet. This, the skeleton fashioned into pipe-length tubes and pierced them for the peace note. Ke-nu placed the reed, then covered them with clay and set them out to dry. As soon as they were ready, the skeleton blew into the holes, making each note one of sweetness and power, working each until each was as sweet as the first. Only then did Ke-nu turn the pipe bowls between thumb and forefinger and join them to the stems. Rising to his feet at last, he bent and placed a pipe in the jaws of each of the skulls that they might have a trail smoke. In return for this courtesy, the skulls gave each pipe great drawing power, which, long afterward, men tried to copy and failed.

Ke-nu gave the sacred pipes to his people. Again there was peace in the village, for after drawing upon the pipes, the skeletons became living men and took wives among the women, who ceased their quarreling. Thus, the cave of the skulls became the cave of the peacemakers.

Skull Cave stack is not as conspicuous as Sugar Loaf. Skull Cave is a crumbling sea stack that has a large amphitheater-like opening. This feature is composed of Mackinac breccia and is the result of glacial Lake Algonquin. The most plausible theory for the formation of the breccia is that salt beds deposited during the Silurian period were dissolved, forming vast caverns into which the overlying Silurian and Devonian limestone beds collapsed and were recemented. The sea stack has a summit of 831 feet above sea level and is between fifteen and twenty-five feet high. It is separated from the headland of the former glacial Lake Algonquin by about fifty feet. Located in the west side of the stack is a sea cave produced by wave action. The entrance to the cave is approximately three feet in diameter and is awash or slightly submerged at the lake's highest level. The cave's interior is pocketed due to erosion in the softer parts of the breccia. The rounding and smoothing of rock surfaces, which characterize wear by waves, are not very evident.

Cave in the Woods

Cave in the Woods is approximately 140 feet above the level of present-day Lake Huron on a prehistoric beach of Lake Algonquin. It was formed by wave action of that ancient lake. It is an amphitheater-shaped opening or sea cave in the Mackinac breccia. The cave floor was rounded as the waves' erosive power cut through the softer material in the limestone mass. Mackinac breccia is composed of masses of rock from many of the described formations. It is not a stratigraphic unit representing a distinct episode of deposition, but is a record of events that involved the fracture and displacement of sedimentary rocks.

Crack in the Island.

Crack in the Island is a crack in the limestone that, at this location, is on the order of about one foot wide and one to two feet deep. Solution cracks occur in several other places on the island. Long fissures or cracks in the limestone surface are common on Mackinac Island. The geological formation was caused by the erosive activity of surface and ground waters. This chemical erosion, known as solution, slowly dissolved the softer rock and left a more resistant brecciated (fractured and recemented) limestone.

The effects of coastline erosion are well recorded in the wave-cut cliffs and abandoned beaches found on the island. The island offers an excellent opportunity to explore shoreline features related to the glacial Lakes Algonquin and Nipissing formed at the edge of the receding continental ice sheets of ten thousand to twelve thousand years ago. Since shoreline features are commonly in unconsolidated material, only the latest events are recorded in these materials, with the earlier features being obliterated by later events. If you wander around up to Fort Holmes, you will find cobbles, pebbles, rocks, and boulders with glacial striations. The glaciers retreated in a northeasterly direction. You will also notice glacial erratics. These are rocks that differ in size and type of rock that is not native to the area that it rests. Basically, it has no earthly business being there. That is the beauty. In addition to being important as a geological site, it is home to about four hundred different species of wildflowers. Many are rare native plants. Mackinac Island's forests contain both conifers (softwoods or evergreens) and northern hardwoods. There is also an abundance of wildlife, including mammals, birds, amphibians, reptiles, insects, and fish.

PICTURES

When I was a private tour driver, I would on occasion get a request for me to take them on a photography cruise, if you will. They wanted to get some real nice pictures, more than they wanted the tour. I explained that the route that I had in mind would take about two hours. The horses that were taking this on our tour from left to right were Carrie and Carmel. I would head through town to Windermere Point, traveling at a speed where they can shoot as we go. I would turn on to Market Street and turn up Cadott toward the Grand Hotel. When we got to the Grand Hotel, we would travel across the front of the Grand Hotel, to the *west end of the front porch*, where they could get a photograph of the full length of the front porch.

Then we would continue on over to West Bluff where we would stop at the *top of the hill in front of the Pines* for another photo opportunity. We would continue along West Bluff and stop in front of Randy and Michelle Stuck's, at the head of Pontiac's Trail, one of the popular stops on the private tour for another photo opportunity.

We would now continue to go through West Bluff and head into the Annex, and instead of going straight, I would make the left where they would have an opportunity to get some pictures of the Straits area and the Mackinac Bridge. As we kept going, we would get to a spot *between the Weiss Cottage and the Lake Cliff Cottage*. Here they would get an awesome picture of the Mackinac Bridge and the Straits area.

We would continue through the Annex, and then we would make a left onto Annex Road. We would follow Annex Road out to the arch over the road out by Stone Cliff. Here we would make a right and follow the road around to where we were *out at the end of the runway for the airport*. Here they would get some beautiful pictures of Saint Ignace, Mackinac Bridge, and the Straits area. Here we would do a three-point turn and head out the way we came in.

We would continue past the barnyard. *When we got to Turkey Hill, we would stop and look to the right over the Jewel* and see a very nice picture of the whole Straits area in general.

We would continue along on Annex Road, go behind the fort, and head on over to East Bluff. Our first stop would be at the head of the trail that would go either down to Marquette Park or up to Anne's Tablet, *by the Lewis Cass Memorial, in front of Crow's Nest, one of the stops on the private tour.* Here they would get an excellent picture of the harbor, Round Island, and the Straits area in general.

We would head down East Bluff; here we would stop *halfway down the bluff, at the steps that take them down to Bogan Lane.* Here they would be able to get a picture of both the fort and the Grand Hotel in the same picture.

We would continue down East Bluff and stop *just before we get to Mission Hill; there are steps that will get them to Harbor View B&B and Sainte Anne's Church.* Here they would get a picture of the Straits Beacon of the west break wall, Round Island Lighthouse, and the steeple of Sainte Anne's Church all in the same picture.

Instead going down Mission Hill, we would go up East Bluff to the access road that goes between two cottages, go down it to Algonquin Trail, make a left, go to the end and make another left, and continue down East Bluff, *until we would get behind Mission Point Resort.* There will be two cedars forming a *V.* Here they could get awesome pictures of MPR, Round Island, Bois Blanc Island, the Straits area, and the Mackinac Bridge. And now with Carrie and Carmel, we would now head back to the park where this all began two hours ago.

Some Other Places for Pictures

Copula Bar at the Grand Hotel

Anne's Tablet

Arch Rock

Backyard at Stone Cliff Mansion

Silver birches on the back side of the island

British Landing

Up at the fort

The First Nations were once very powerful. At one time, they could take care of themselves. A lot of their trails were followed and paved over as our highway system. As time progressed, they became more dependent. They became dependent on the gunpowder, ammunition, blankets, tomahawks, knives, a lot of the stuff they used for hunting—the lead ball could travel a lot faster and farther than an arrow—and some of the clothing that they wore. And they realized that. This brought about problems when the traders were not allowed to sell to the First Nations.

With the fur trade, we had the missionaries fighting with the fur traders over rum being given to the natives. Missionaries get thrown out of the territory. During the fur trade, they became more dependent upon the white man for all their needs. The French had an amicable relationship with the natives. The British, on the other hand, treated them as third-class citizens and often cheated them. Michigan Territory was center stage for the fur trade. The French arrived first, then the French and the British went at it in a mini French and Indian war before it began. The British took over after their winning the French and Indian war, getting the holdings of everything east of the Mississippi. The British and Americans were competing for the coveted fur. Then with the War of 1812, the British were kicked out of the United States. All we have left is the American Fur Company.

The fur trade industry went through some transitions. A lot of these transitions were with the way in which the countries France and England dealt with each other and also the way they dealt with the First Nations. They had to deal with nefarious miscreants, and at times they were just as corrupt as the people they were dealing with. Being on the other side of the pond and trying to enforce the rules did not help matters any.

One of the biggest transitions was from independent to companies. This was going throughout the fur trade, then going from two companies to one huge company. This would go on until about 1834 when the fur trade moved west with the expansion of the country.

The fur trade brought one of the most influential women to the island, Magdelaine LaFramboise. She was of mixed with Odawa and French blood. She and her husband were big in the fur trade down in the Ada, Michigan, area. Her husband, Joseph, was murdered by a native. She would throw a social, and Dr. Beaumont would be present. She did a lot for Mackinac Island. She was a teacher and businesswoman, donating property so that Sainte Anne's could be moved to the east end of the island. Sainte Anne's went about sixty-five years without a priest. It is the oldest Catholic congregation dedicated to Sainte Anne in North America, with three hundred years' worth of baptismal records dating back to 1695.

With the fur trade, we also get the forts. Three flags have flown over the forts at one time or another, the French, the British, and the American. It was first located over in Saint Ignace; it was run by the French. Then the French moved it to the south side of the Straits. After the British won the Seven Years' War, they took over the fort. With the American Revolution, the British commander did not like his position. The fort was located in proximity to the lake, making it hard to defend. With the signing of Michigan's first treaty, they moved the fort across the Straits to the heights overlooking the Straits on Mackinac Island.

The fort, as a fortification, seems to be a mixture of American frontier post and old-world castle. The thick walls and sally ports, bastions and ditch, its four old blockhouses of logs, the powder magazines located near the east sally port, loopholes for muskets, sloping path down to the village, buttressed along the hillside with heavy masonry—all these make it sort of a mountain fortress, something you find in the countryside in Europe.

The fort was an active-duty post until 1870, then from 1870 to 1895, the fort was run by the National Park Service. After 1895, it was sold to the state of Michigan, making it the state's first state park. With the fort came Dr. Beaumont, who did his study of the human digestive system with the help of his patient Alexis St. Martin.

With the loss of the fur trade, they were searching for an industry. For a while it was the fishing industry. Along with fishing came the coopers to build the barrels to put the fish in. That lasted for a while, then the candy makers came, for the weather was conducive to making candy. The fudge came after WWI. In July 1882, the Grand Hotel opened its doors. The tourist industry had arrived. The island and the Grand Hotel had what I would refer to as a symbiotic relationship. They need each other to survive. Some great authors have also visited Mackinac Island—Alexis de Tocqueville, Mark Twain, Constance Fenimore Woolson, and Henry David Thoreau, to name a few. What a list.

Doing something like a photography shoot or a wedding was always enjoyable for the driver and the horses. It was kind of weird, but I think the two horses in the team enjoyed it as much as the driver. Those two horses would know that we were doing something other than a tour. I think they knew something different was going on when we made our left on to Annex Road. That was usually when I would see a little excitement in their demeanor. It was as exciting for them as it was for me. That was the reason I loved the private tour so much. I was not doing the same thing all the time.

The sweetest team that I had the privilege of ever driving was Carrie and Carmel. They were definitely low maintenance. When we were doing weddings, Carrie would hold her neck, proud, and Carmel would always be looking around for the camera, and more times than not, she would usually find it. I do not know how she managed to find that silly camera.

Backing a carriage was a nightmare for me, because I am dyslexic. I had to always stop and think about which way I had to move the horses in order to get the carriage to go in the direction I want it to go—haw, left; gee, right; woo, stop. Those two taught me a lot about trusting the team. One time I was backing my livery in, and within a few minutes, we had it. At this time, my cousin Donny Houghton was barnman up at the infamous barn 4. He was heading up the team while I unhooked the horses from the carriage. While I was walking the team, we were talking, and he mentioned to me that I should listen to my horses more, because when

I was backing up, they were looking as to where the carriage was going. What a wonderful lesson. The end of the day was even faster after that. They knew where I wanted that carriage.

I never fed my teams from my hand; I saw it as a bad habit for the horses to get into. I would discourage the public from doing it as well. I would have them give me the apple, and then I would make sure they got it at the end of the day. Then I would cut it in half and put it in with their other feed. If I had an apple that I had left over from my day off, which was always, I would cut it in half and then put it in with their feed. I was probably the biggest jerk down in the park when it came to letting the public pet the horses. The answer was always no.

One time I was picking a private tour group at the ticket office. I had just told about ten people no to petting my horses. Along came this woman who asked if she could pet my horses. I told her, "No, sorry, they are on the job and working." She blew up and emphatically told me she was a horse trainer. I told her that she, of all people, should know better, because they were working. She did not like the answer. So I asked her if it would it be all right for me to leave the stands at a horse show and pet a horse in the arena. I knew the answer is no. Besides, there were ten people over on the sidewalk, watching as I told her no. If I let her, I would have a riot on my hands.

Another livery team that I enjoyed driving was Pogo and Bess. People were convinced that Bess was a witch, but Pogo brought some of his own problems on himself some of the time. Pogo, I believe, was Morgan/draft. He had the color of a Morgan; his head was small in proportion to his body. Finding a halter or bridle to fit that small head was difficult. In one day, one summer, he slipped his bridle three times. The third time he did it, Dr. Bill was riding by on his bike. I asked him if he would take a look at what was going on. We figured out what he was doing; we needed a chin strap. All I had on me was a hames strap. I gave it to him, and in no time, the problem was solved. Then he was asking where I got my hames strap. I explained to him what Johnny Thompson told me once. Seventy-five percent of harness problems could be solved with a hames strap. I always had one with me. For livery, the hames strap was kind of gaudy, but it worked. One of the barnmen fixed me up a chin strap that looked real sharp for livery.

It was not just bridles he would slip. At night he would slip his halter. In the morning, he would be in his stall, having turned around, greeting you face-to-face. One of the funniest things that I had ever seen happen to a horse—the situation was not funny; it was the sight—was one time in the morning, I beat the barnman to barn 4, like normal, to get my team ready for the day. I was walking through the barn, looking and talking to the horses as I was walking down the aisle. Out of the corner of my eye, I saw a sight; it was kind of funny yet unbelievable. Bess had somehow gotten on her back, but she could not get upright. I do not know if the stall was too small for her or what. I climbed over her stall and first unhooked the lead rope so she did not hurt herself in any way while getting up. It was going to take more than two people to pull her out of that stall. There were three of us. We managed to get her out into the aisle, and thankfully, with a little prodding, she was able to get up. It was kind of a funny sight. You have to understand her temperament to really appreciate the circumstances. Just the sight of old Bess on her back with all four legs in the air made my day.

Michigan is fortunate in that it has three crown jewels of the Great Lakes. All three are islands. First is Beaver Island. You can take your automobile over there by catching the ferry in Charlevoix. Next, we have Isle Royale; it is an island in the middle of Lake Superior. It is a national park. This jewel cannot handle the people traffic; it will be wrecked. Then we have Mackinac Island. All freight and mail is delivered by dray. The only authorized motorized vehicles are ambulance, police car, fire trucks, snowmobile—the main mode of transportation in the wintertime—and maintenance vehicles. That is the beauty of this gem.

When you go visit the island, there is a lot to do. Take a tour, public or private, walk, and explore the interior of the island. There are a lot of real interesting day trips you can do as well. The night life is different on the island. When that last boat leaves for the day, the island becomes quiet. If you do stay over on the island and you reside in either downstate, I would say Saginaw, Michigan, south, unless you live in the country away from the city lights, you can convince yourself there are no stars in the lower evening sky. What I am trying to say is make sure you get out and look up in the lower evening sky; it is incredible. Bottom line is, when you go, relax and have fun. In the end, Mackinac Island is a huge chunk of limestone in the middle of Lake Huron, two miles in circumference, with seventy to eighty miles of hiking, biking, and equestrian trails for your pleasure and enjoyment. Eighty percent of the island is owned and operated by the state park. If you were to take the tour, you will probably be in and out of the state park seven or eight times throughout the tour.

BIBLIOGRAPHY

Andrews, Roger. *Old Fort Mackinac on the Hill of History.* Menominee, MI: Herald Leader Press, 1938.

Artman, Carolyn. "Carriages on Mackinac Island." *Where the Horse Is King.* Mackinac Memories. Mackinac Island State Park Centennial 1895–1995. Commemorative Program. Mackinac Island State Park Commission, 1998 and 1999. http://www.hal.state.mi.us/mhc/autoshow/vehicles/carriage.html.

ASCE (American Society of Civil Engineers). "Straits of Mackinac, Michigan, Constructed between 1954 and 1957." http://www.asce.org/People-and-Projects/Projects/Landmarks/Mackinac-Bridge/.

Bay City Times. "True North: The Magazine of Northeast Michigan Living." June/July 2008.

Bersey, John. "William Westover." *Cyclopedia of Michigan: Historical and Biographical, Comprising a Synopsis.* New York and Detroit: Western Publishing and Engraving Co. Entered according to act of Congress in the year 1890 by John Bersey in the Office of the Library of Congress at Washington, DC.

Biography. "John Jacob Astor." The Biography.com website. Accessed July 3, 2015. http://www.biography.com/people/john-jacob-astor-9191158.

Biography. "William Backhouse Astor" (2015). The Biography.com website. Retrieved 3:32, July 3, 2015. http://www.biography.com/people/william-backhouse-astor-9191266.

Boynton, James. *Fishers of Men: The Jesuit Mission at Mackinac 1670–1765.* Ste. Anne's Church, 1996.

Busch, Anheuser. "Clydesdale Facts." http://anheuser-busch.com/index. php/our-heritage/budweiser-clydesdales/budweiser-clydesdale-facts/.

Delaney, Jessica. "Boy Scouts Clean Up Round Island Light." Front page. *Town Crier.* August 27, 2005.

D'Entremont, Jeremy. "History of Boston Light, Massachusetts." http:// www.newenglandlighthouses.net/boston-light-history.html.

Encyclopedia. "Astor, John Jacob." *UXL Encyclopedia of World Biography.* 2003. Encyclopedia.com. Accessed July 3, 2015. http://www. encyclopedia.com/doc/1G2-3437500055.html.

Epstein, Sam, and Beryl Epstein. *Dr. Beaumont and the Man with a Hole in His Stomach.* Coward McCann & Geoghegan Inc., 1978.

Gringhuis, Dirk, author and illustrator. *Lore of the Great Turtle: Indian Legends of Mackinac Retold.* Mackinac Island State Historical Parks, 1970.

Hamil, Fred C. *When Beaver Was King.* Wayne University Press, 1951.

Hamilton, R. N. *Father Marquette.* William B. Eerdmans Publishing Company.

Hoogterp, Edward. "Lighthouse Design, Michigan Lighthouse Conservancy." Night Lights. Travel section. *Saginaw News*, Sunday, April 20, 2008.

Johnson, Ida Amanda. *The Michigan Fur Trade.* Grand Rapids, MI: Black Letter Press. First published 1919 by the Michigan Historical Commission. Authorized reprinting 1971, 1975, and 1981.

Kelton, Dwight H. *Annals of Fort Mackinac.* Detroit Free Press Printing Co. 1888.

Knoll, Denys W. *Battle of Lake Erie: Building the Fleet in the Wilderness.* Washington, DC: Naval Historical Foundation, Spring 1979.

Lighthouse Friends. "Point Betsie Lighthouse." http://www. lighthousefriends.com/light.asp?id=199.

Mackinac Bridge Authority. "Mackinac Bridge Information." Designed and produced by Gaslight Media, 2000–2012.

Mackinac Island State Historical Parks. "Mackinac Island's Post Cemetery." *Mackinac History Illustrated Vignettes.* Vol. III, leaflet no. 3. 1999.

Mackinac Island State Park Commission. "Post Cemetery." Mackinac Island State Park Media. 2013.

Mackinac Island Town Crier. June16, 2007. Copyright 2005–2012.

Maranzani, Barbara. "America's First Multi-Millionaire." The History. com webpage. Retrieved 8:46, July 18, 2015. http://www.history.com/ news/americas-first-multi-millionaire-250-years-later.

Marsh, James. *First Nations and the War of 1812.* N.d., n.p. Web November 12, 2014. The Royal Canadian Geographical Society and Parks Canada, 2011.

May, George S. *War of 1812: The United States and Great Britain at Mackinac, 1812–1815.* Mackinac State Historical Park Commission, 1962, 1970, 2004.

McCabe, John. *Grand Hotel.* Sault Sainte Marie, MI: The Unicorn Press, Lake Superior State University, 1987.

Michigan Historical Center. "Father Marquette's Journal." *Michigan History Magazine.* 3rd ed. 2001.

Milstein, Randall L. "Geological Society of America Centennial Field Guide—North-Central Section, 1987." Mackinac Island State Park, Michigan. Subsurface and Petroleum Geology Unit, Michigan Geological Survey, Lansing, Michigan. Michigan.gov/documents/ deq/GIMDL-GSA87I_302413_7.pdf.

National Park Service. "The National Park Service: History of the National Park." www.cr.nps.gov/history/hisnps/NPSHistory/npshisto.htm.

Olson, David J. "The Mackinac Bridge." http://www.michigan.gov/dnr/0,4570,7-153-54463_18670_18793-53649--,00.html.

Pepper, Terry. "Keeper of the Island." *Seeing the Light.* http://www.terrypepper.com/lights/huron/roundisland/keepers.htm.

Pepper, Terry. "Round Island Light." *Seeing the Light.* www.terrypepper.com/Lights/huron/roundisland/roundisland.htm.

Porter, Phil. *The Wonder of Mackinac: A Guide to the Natural History of Mackinac Island.* Illustrated by Victor R. Nelhiebel. Mackinac Island State Park Commission, 1984.

Porter, Phil. *View from the Veranda.* 2nd ed. Mackinac Island State Park Commission, 2006.

Rethford, Wayne. "The Zenith Corporation—Founded by Eugene F. McDonald." *Scots Great and Small, People and Places.* http://chicagoscots.blogspot.com/2012/01/zenith-corporation-founded-by-eugene-f.html.

Rural Heritage. "What is a Draft Horse: Belgian, Clydesdale, Percheron." July 5, 2006. Last revision October 19, 2011 last revision. http://ruralheritage.com/horse_paddock/index.htm.

Sage, Ronald P., and Victoria L. Sage. "Glacial Lakes Algonquin and Nipissing Shoreline Bedrock Features: Mackinac Island, Michigan." *Field Trip Guidebook.* Vol. 52, part 2. Sault Sainte Marie, Ontario: Institute on Lake Superior Geology, 2006. www.d.umn.edu/prc/.../ILSG_52_2006_pt2_Sault_Ste_Marie.cv.PDF.

Shire, Jesse. *Life and Letters of Dr. Beaumont.* C. V. Mosby, 1912.

Smith, Corinnee Horsfeld. *Westward I Go Free: Tracing Thoreau's Last Journey.* Green Frigate Books, 2012.

Straus, Frank. "Old Courthouse Dispenses Justice for 170 Years on Mackinac Island." A Look at History. *Mackinac Island Town Crier.* www.mackinacislandnews.com.

Straus, Frank. "Key Legal Precedents Are Set in Mackinac Island's Historic Courthouse." A Look at History. *Mackinac Island Town Crier.* www. mackinacislandnews.com.

Sullivan, Jack. "David Hogg and Alexander Hannah." <u>*Those Pre-Pro Whiskey Men!*</u> http://pre-prowhiskeymen.blogspot.com/2013/07/ hannah-hogg-sowed-thistles-in-chicago.html.

Tagartz, Bob, narrator. "History of the Grand Hotel." Grand Hotel, 2008. DVD.

Taylor, Paul. "Engineered To Endure: The Great Lakes Lighthouses of Orlando Poe." *Michigan History.* Vol. 8, no. 5. September/October 2014. Historical Society of Michigan, 2014.

Todish, Timothy J., and Todd E. Harburn. *A "Most Troublesome Situation": The British Military and the Pontiac Uprising of 1763–1764.* Art by Robert Griffing and Gary Zaboly. New York: Purple Mountain Press Fleischmann's, 2006.

Triposo. "Mackinac Bridge." https://www.triposo.com/poi/ Mackinac_Bridge.

Waldorf Astoria New York. "Over a Century of History and Unique Heritage." http://www.waldorfnewyork.com/

Widder, Keith R. "Magdelaine Laframboise: The First Lady of Mackinac Island." *Michigan History.* Vol. 4, leaflet no. 1. 2007.

Williams, Meade C. *The Best Book about the Island Mackinac.* New York: Duffield & Company, 1912.

Wilson, Jayne D. "Breed Profile: Belgian Draft Horse." *EQUUS.* Cruz Bay Publishing Inc., 2014. http://www.equisearch.com/resources/breeds/ belgianprofile/.

Index

A

Abbott, Samuel, 82
Akashi Kaikyo Bridge, 115
American Bridge Company, 113
American Fur Company, 50–51,
   61–63
Annex, 40, 102–4, 123–24, 126,
   152–53, 156
armorers, 14
Armstrong, Mac, 21
Arnold Line, 3, 94–95, 97
Astor, John Jacob, 60–63
Astor, John Jacob, II, 62–63
Astor, John Jacob, IV, 64
Astor, William Backhouse, 62–63

B

Ballard, J. Logan, 107
Battle of Lake Erie, 80, 90, 160
Battle of Logwoods, 86
Bazinaw, Joe, 4
Beaumont, William, 49–51, 160
Bidagan, Joseph Pierre, 50
bladesmith, 14
Blagojevich, Rod, 5
Blanchard, Isaac, 66
Bois Blanc Island, 45, 77, 79, 86, 115
Brighten Pavilion, 108

Brown, James, 66
Budweiser Clydesdale, 25, 29
Burbeck, Henry, 78–79
Burr, Aaron, 62
Busch, Adolphus, III, 25
Busch, August A., 25
Busch, August A., Sr., 25
Butler, Anthony, 89

C

Campbell, James V., 66
Caskey, Charles W., 104–5
Cass, Lewis, 153
Chambers, Bill, 27, 32–33
Chambers Corner, 1, 3
Chandler, Benjamin, 49
Charelton, Edward, 78
Chippewas, 72, 74–75, 82, 142
Cliff Cottage, 121, 152
Clowes, George, 78
Clydesdale, 22–26, 28–29
Columbia River Trading Post, 61
Crazy Horse, 70
Cripps, Frank, 14, 16
Cripps, Keith, 14, 16
Croghan, George, 86–88
Crow's Nest, 153
Cupola Bar, 110–11
Custer, George Armstrong, 70

D

Dablon, Claude, 35, 67
Dalmatian, 25–26
Davenport, Ambrose, 82
Day, Sylvester, 81
de la Cadillac, Antoine, 69
DePeyster, A. S., 57, 75
Detroit and Cleveland Steamship
    Navigation Company, 103
de Villeraye, M., 67
diligence horse, 24
Dobbins, Dan, 83–85
Dousman, John, 82
Dousman, Michael, 81
Dray Barn, 16–17
Du Charme, Laurent, 72

E

Eckert, Allan, 5
Etherington, George, 70, 72

F

farriers, 8, 13–16, 37
Ferry, William, 42
Festival of the Horse, 28
First Nations, 36, 53, 55–60, 67–73,
    75–84, 86–88, 90–91, 102
Fitzgerald, Edmund, 43–44
fly predators, 27
Forrest, Georgearm, 31
Fort Astoria, 61–62
Fort Bliss, 50
Fort Collins, 25
Fort De Baude, 67
Fort Detroit, 69, 71, 75–76, 81, 83
Fort George, 86–87
Fort Hill, 20
Fort Mackinac, 41, 50, 59, 66, 77–81,
    83–84, 86–88, 91, 93, 105, 160
Fort Michilimackinac, 70, 72–76
Fort Niagara, 74
Fort Repentigny, 71
Fort Sackville, 76
Fort Saint Ignace, 67–69
Fort Saint Joseph, 71, 73
Franklin, Benjamin, 80
Fuller, Silas, 49

G

George (king), 70–71, 86
Gillespie, Robert, 9
Gladwin (major), 71
Grand Hotel, 16, 27–28, 93, 102–12,
    161
Grand Rapids and Indiana Railroad,
    103–4
Grant's Farm, 25
Great Belt Bridge, 115
Greysolon, Daniel, 68
Guibeau, Marie Des Agnes Angelique,
    50

H

Hanks, Porter, 80–83, 89
Hayes, James Reddington, 106
Hemlock, 43, 95
Henry, Alexander, 72–74
Hivernants, 55
Holman, Ed, 5
Holmes, Andrew Hunter, 86–87
Horn, Tom, 14
Howard, Lewis, 80
Howard, William, 74
Hubbard, Elizabeth, 40
Hubbard, Gurdon, 40, 102–3
Hubbard, Marvin, 9, 12
Hudson Bay Company, 55, 61–62

I

ice bridge, 95–98, 105
Ignatius Loyola, 35
International Lilac Society, 31

J

Jamet, John, 71
Jay Treaty, 58, 61, 78
John Paul XXIII, 39
Johnson, William, 72, 75
Jolliet, Louis, 36

K

King, Stella, 33

L

La Chance, Eugene, 107
Lafitte, Pierre, 86
LaFramboise, Magdelaine, 37–39, 42, 51
Lake Cliff Cottage, 152
Lake Erie, 80, 84–85, 90, 160
Lake Huron, 36, 45–46, 52, 54, 67, 69, 77, 79, 86, 90, 97, 131, 141–43, 146, 150
Lake Michigan, 55, 72, 77
Lake Superior, 43–45, 52, 55, 58–59
Langlade, Charles, 72
Lawrence, 85, 87
Lenox, James, 63
Lighthouse Keepers Association, 47
Lilac Festival, 28, 30, 33
Lilac Queens, 33
Little Barn, 28
Little Stone Church, 40
locksmiths, 14
Louisiana Purchase, 90
Lowell, Joseph, 50

M

Mackinac Bridge, 113–16, 163
Mackinac Bridge Authority, 113
Main Street, 1–2, 4
Marquette, 36, 153, 160–61
Marquette, Jacques, 36, 67
Marquette Park, 32
Massay, Ebenezer, 79
McDouall, Robert, 85
McGwire, Mary, 32
Meade, George, 84, 92, 163
Michael, John, 79
Michigan Central Railroad, 103
Mission Church, 40, 42
Moore, Benjamin, 49
Mosley, Ben, 28
Musser, Dan, 109–10

N

Newark Brewery, 25
Niagara, 73–75, 84–85, 88
North West Company, 58–59, 61–62

P

Percheron, 22–25, 27–28, 162
Perrot, Nicolas, 68
Peterson, Dale, vii, 9, 12
Petit, Jim, 16–17
Pickford, 95, 100
Plank, John Oliver, 106
Poe, Orlando M., 45
Point Betsie Lighthouse, 44
Pond, Augustus, 66
Pontiac, 55, 70–73, 95, 152
Porter, Hanks, 80–83, 89
Powell, Truman, 49
Prior, Abner, 79
Prohibition, 25, 107–8
Pullman, George, 103

R

Rezek, Antoine, 39
Robertson, Daniel, 78
Robinson's Folly, 142
Rogers, Robert, 74–75
Roosevelt, Franklin Delano, 25

Round Island Lighthouse, 43–44, 46–47

Ruluson, Dick, 1–4

S

Sainte Anne's Church, 35, 153

Saint Joseph Island, 81, 86, 88

Salina, 83–84

Schuberg, Eric, 14

Schwann, Theodor, 50

Scorpion, 88–89

Sibinic, Allan, 27

Sinclair, Arthur, 86

Sinclair, Patrick, 36, 76–77, 95

Six Nations, 60

Solomon, Ezekiel, 57

Steinman, David B., 113, 115

St. Martin, Alexis, 49–51

Stockbridge, Francis B., 103

St. Onge, Jason, 96

Straits of Mackinac, 36, 46, 52

Surrey Hill, 2–3, 5, 9, 27, 32

T

Tacoma Narrows Bridge, 115

Thompson, Johnny, 12

Thoreau, Henry David, 31

Tigress, 88–89

Tilden, Samuel, 63

Todd, Sarah Cox, 61

Topam, Brenda, 21

Trail of Tears, 91

Treaty of Ghent, 89

Treaty of Paris, 58, 65, 78, 80

Trinity Church, 20, 40–41

V

Van Renterghem, Henri, 37

Van Wagoner, Murray D., 113

Varney, Colton, 110

von Steuben, Friedrich, 69

W

War of 1812, *49–50, 59, 61, 80, 85, 90, 91*, 161

Wawatum, 73–74

Weaver, Henry, 107

WEST BLUFF, 113

white nose syndrome, 27

Wilson, Ernest Henry, 31

Woodfill, W. Stewart, 107–9

Woodfill Memorial, 1–2

Wright, Tom, 10

Y

Yankee Rebel, 82

Printed in the United States
By Bookmasters